Insiders 11-14

Inside English

Steve Eddy
Shelagh Hubbard
Adrian Tissier

Contents

Introduction iv
Inside English and the National Curriculum iv
How this book works vi

The Basics of English

About Spoken English
Accent and Dialect 2
Informal and Formal Register 4
How Spoken Language Changes 6
Differences Between Speech and Writing 8

Spelling
English Word Roots 10
Spelling Rules 12
Better Spelling 14
Using a Dictionary and Thesaurus 16
Sounds and Syllables 18

Grammar
Nouns, Articles and Adjectives 20
Pronouns and Noun Phrases 22
Verbs, Adverbs and Prepositions 24
Verbs - Tenses and Phrases 26
Simple and Compound Sentences 28
Complex Sentences 30

Punctuation of Sentences
Commas and Full Stops 32
Apostrophes, Colons and Semi-colons 34
Inverted commas 36
Paragraphs 38

Authoring Skills
Reasons for Writing 40
Planning your Writing 42
Proofreading and Presentation 44

Speaking and Listening
Be a Better Listener 46
Interviewing 48
Group Work 50
Confidence in Front of an Audience 52
Making a Persuasive Speech 54

Reading and Writing: Non-fiction

Study Skills
Skimming, Scanning and Close Reading	56
Using the Library	58
Research from Information Texts	60
Making Notes and Summaries	62

Basic Information Texts
Charts, Graphs and Tables	64
Writing Instructions	66
Texts Combining Words and Pictures	68
Writing a Report	70

Letters
Writing a Letter	72
Letters to the Editor	74

Reviews
Reading and Comparing Reviews	76
Writing Reviews	78

Newspapers
News Reports	80
Facts and Opinions	82
Bias	84
Writing a News Feature	86

Leaflets and Adverts
Understanding Adverts	88
Writing Adverts	90
Charity Appeals	92
Warnings and Advice	94

Reading and Writing: Literature

Literary Non-fiction
Diaries and Letters	96
Biography and Autobiography	98
Travel Writing	100

Short Stories and Novels
Reading Modern Prose	102
Reading Older Prose	104
Myths	106
Legends	108
Character Description	110
Plot and Theme	112
Setting and Atmosphere	114
Narrative Technique and the Author's Voice	116
Writing Your Own Short Story	118

Poems
Reading a Modern Poem	120
Reading an Older Poem	122
Sounds and Images	124
Rhyme and Rhythm	126
Writing About a Poem	128
Writing Your Own Poems	130

Plays
Reading a Modern Play	132
Writing Dialogue and Script	134

Shakespeare
Reading Shakespeare	136
Shakespeare's Language	138
Writing About Shakespeare's Characters	140
More About Shakespeare's Characters	142

Common word confusions	144
Mini-thesaurus	145
Further reading	146
Glossary	148
Index	152

Introduction

What Inside English does

- This book is a companion to the English you will do at Key Stage 3 from Year 7 to Year 9. It breaks the course down into all the topic areas you will cover in school and discusses all the most important ideas you need to understand.
- Each double-page spread covers one English topic. Each spread is organised in the same way. The information on each spread will give you a clear guide to that topic.
- Pages vi and vii will show you how each topic works.
- Each spread starts with an introduction to the topic and finishes with a summary of the key points and a question section.

How Inside English can help you

- The book will help you with your English homework by providing all the essential information on every English topic for you to refer to and to help you understand the work.
- You can also use the book to help you with your classwork. When you cover a topic in school you can use the book to help you with any problems and to give you a better understanding of that topic. It can also help you with any work that you miss.
- The book helps you with revision for tests by covering all the key areas you will be tested in. The summaries on every spread will remind you of the key points and you can use the questions in Sections A and B to check that you understand these key ideas.

Inside English and the National Curriculum

English in the National Curriculum

The National Curriculum describes the English you will learn in school. English is split up into three 'Attainment Targets' which describe the different skills you learn. These three attainment targets are:

- Speaking and Listening
- Reading
- Writing

Even though they are different parts of the curriculum, in real life you will often practise them together.

AT1 Speaking and Listening

This is about becoming a more confident speaker of English and a more careful listener. You will practise these skills in pairs and in bigger groups, listening to others and talking about a wide range of things. You will practise talking for different reasons: to discuss things you have experienced and things you have read, to explain your ideas about particular topics, to develop new ideas and to persuade other people to agree with your point of view.

You are not tested on this skill in the Year 9 tests, but your teacher will give you a level based on the speaking and listening you have done in school.

AT2 Reading

This is about becoming a more skilful and more experienced reader. You will read a wide variety of texts, for example: poems, short stories, novels, plays, magazines and leaflets. You will also watch films and television programmes.

Your teacher will give you a level based on the reading you do in the lessons and in your own time. For your Year 9 test you will read and study closely one of Shakespeare's plays. You will also have to answer questions about some unfamiliar shorter texts that will be given to you in the test.

AT3 Writing

This is about becoming a more skilful and more careful writer of English. You will practise writing for different purposes and for different readers. A lot of your written work will be about the literature texts you are reading.

For your Year 9 test you will study and write about one of Shakespeare's plays, and you will also answer questions about some unfamiliar shorter texts.

Language study in the three attainment targets

As well as becoming a better user of English, you will also learn more about how the English language works during Key Stage 3. For example:

- In AT1 you will study how the grammar and vocabulary of local dialects is different from what is called 'Standard English'.
- In AT2 you will learn more about special uses of language in literature and media texts.
- In AT3 you will learn more about grammar and punctuation.

This book is about all the things you have to cover in Attainment Targets 1, 2 and 3. You can use it throughout Key Stage 3 to help you understand the course and to help you with your homework and your classwork.

Inside English and the Key Stage 3 Tests

What are the Key Stage 3 Tests?
Science, Maths and English are the core subjects of the National Curriculum. You will be tested in these in May during Year 9.

When the tests are marked by external markers (not your teacher) you will be given a 'level' for your work. The levels you reach in the Key Stage 3 tests are sent to your parents and the overall results for each school are also published in the form of league tables.

What are Levels?
The National Curriculum gives teachers a way of measuring your achievement by describing nine different 'levels' for each attainment target. The levels describe the kind of knowledge and understanding you should have at each level. In English you should be working at a level between 3 and 7 at the end of Key Stage 3, although some students might achieve Level 8 or even the 'Exceptional Performance' level.

What are Teacher Assessments?
Your teacher will measure your progress in English towards the end of Year 9, and give you a level for the work and tests you have done in school.

How can I use this book for revision?
As well as helping you throughout Years 7, 8 and 9, you can use this book to help you with your revision for the tests.

Everybody has their own way of revising before tests and examinations, and you should revise in a way that suits you. As a starting point, you can use the summaries and quick Section A questions on every spread to quickly test your basic understanding of a topic.

How this book works

Writing Your Own Short Story

When writing a story you need to think about how to make it interesting, and what you want your readers to feel when they read it.

These pages are about helping you to write your own stories.

Notice how Dylan Thomas has used a [range] of unusual descriptive words to make [the] setting and the characters come alive.

Planning
When you want to write a story you will need to start off with a plan to help you make the most of your ideas and to make the story interesting for anyone who reads it.

In your plan it is a good idea to make some headings where you can note down the different ideas you have. Of course you may want to change these ideas later as the story develops. Your headings should include the following:

- **Plot and theme**
  What is going to happen in the story?
  What is it going to be about?
- **Characters**
  How many characters will there be? (You may not want to have too many characters or it might be confusing.) Is the reader meant to like/dislike them? Will they be realistic/fantasy/cartoons/animals?
- **Narrative**
  Will it be written in first or third person narrative? Is it going to be exciting/tense/descriptive? Do you want the readers to laugh or cry or be frightened?
- **Setting**
  Where and when will the story be set?

Drafting and revising
Using your plan you can now write the first draft of your story. This is an opportunity for you to try out different ideas and to experiment with words and style.

When you read over what you have written you can then make changes, crossing things out and adding other details according to what you want your story to do. After you have revised your story carefully, you will be able to write the final version.

Read the following opening to a story by the twentieth-century writer Dylan Thomas. Try to see what he has done to make the story lively and unusual.

In the middle of the night I woke from a dream full of whips and lariats as long as serpents, and runaway coaches on mountain passes, and wide, windy gallops over cactus fields, and I heard the man in the next room crying, 'Gee-up!' and 'Whoa!' and trotting his tongue on the roof of his mouth.

It was the first time I had stayed in grandpa's house. The floorboards had squeaked like mice as I climbed into bed, and the mice between the walls had creaked like wood as though another visitor was walking on them. It was a mild summer night, but curtains had flapped and branches beaten against the window. I had pulled the sheets over my head, and soon was roaring and riding in a book.

'Whoa there my beauties!' cried grandpa. His voice sounded very young and loud, and his tongue had powerful hooves, and he made his bedroom into a great meadow. I thought I would see if he was ill, or had set his bedclothes on fire, for my mother had said that he lit his pipe under the blankets, and had warned me to run to his help if I smelt smoke in the night. I went on tiptoe through the darkness to his bedroom door, brushing against the furniture and upsetting a candlestick with a thump.

When I saw there was a light in the room I felt frightened, and as I opened the door I heard grandpa shout, 'Gee-up!' as loudly as a bull with a megaphone.

He was sitting straight up in bed and rocking from side to side as though the bed were on a rough road; the knotted edges of the counterpane were his reins; his invisible horse stood in a shadow beyond the bedside candle. Over a white flannel nightshirt he was wearing a red waistcoat with walnut-sized brass buttons. The over-filled bowl of his pipe smouldered among his whiskers like a little burning hayrick on a stick. At the sight of me, his hands dropped from the reins and lay blue and quiet, the bed stopped still on a level road, he muffled his tongue into silence, and the horses drew softly up.

'Is there anything the matter, grandpa?' I asked, though the clothes were not on fire. His face in the candlelight looked like a ragged quilt pinned upright on the black air and patched all over with goat-beards.

He stared at me mildly. Then he blew down [his pipe,] sparks and making a high, wet dog whistle of [steam.] 'Ask no questions.'

After a pause he said slyly: 'Do you ever hav[e a cake?]' I said: 'No.'
'Oh yes, you do,' he said.
I said I was woken by a voice that was shou[ting.]
'What did I tell you?' he said. 'You eat too m[uch.] Who ever heard of horses in a bedroom?'

He fumbled under his pillow, brought out a small, tinkling bag and carefully untied its strings. He put a sovereign in my hand, and said: 'Buy a cake.' I thanked him and wished him good night.

As I closed my bedroom door, I heard his voice crying loudly and gaily.

from *A Visit to Grandpa's* by Dylan Thomas

118

For more information about the techniques of stor[y...]

Introduction
This gives you a starting-point for the topic and some of the ideas that you will want to think about first.

Learning objectives
This tells you what part of your course is covered in this topic. It is your quick guide to the content of the two pages.

Cross-references
This provides you with links to other pages where you can find out more about ideas contained in this topic.

How this book works

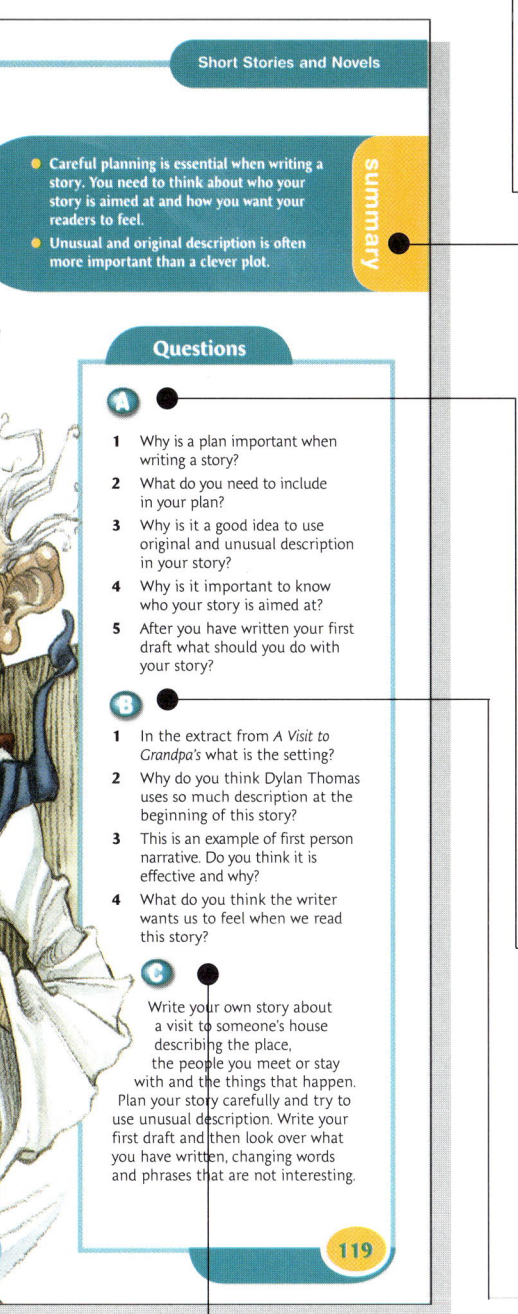

Interesting Facts and Helpful Hints.
This box is a Helpful Hint box. It gives you a special tip or some extra ideas to help you with the topic.

Another box you will see from time to time is the Interesting Fact box. It has a symbol which looks like this:

Summary
The Summary gives you a checklist of all the key points on the topic. You can use it while you are working on the topic to check that you have understood the work, or you can use it when you revise as a guide to the main points.

Quick questions
The questions in Section A are quick questions. You can use them to quickly test that you understand the topic either when you cover it during your course or when you revise.

Main questions
The Section B questions are your main question resource. These questions cover the different areas of the topic and allow you to check that you can answer questions about all these different areas.

Further questions
The Section C questions provide you with some additional work to take the topic a bit further. You may have to use other resources to answer these questions.

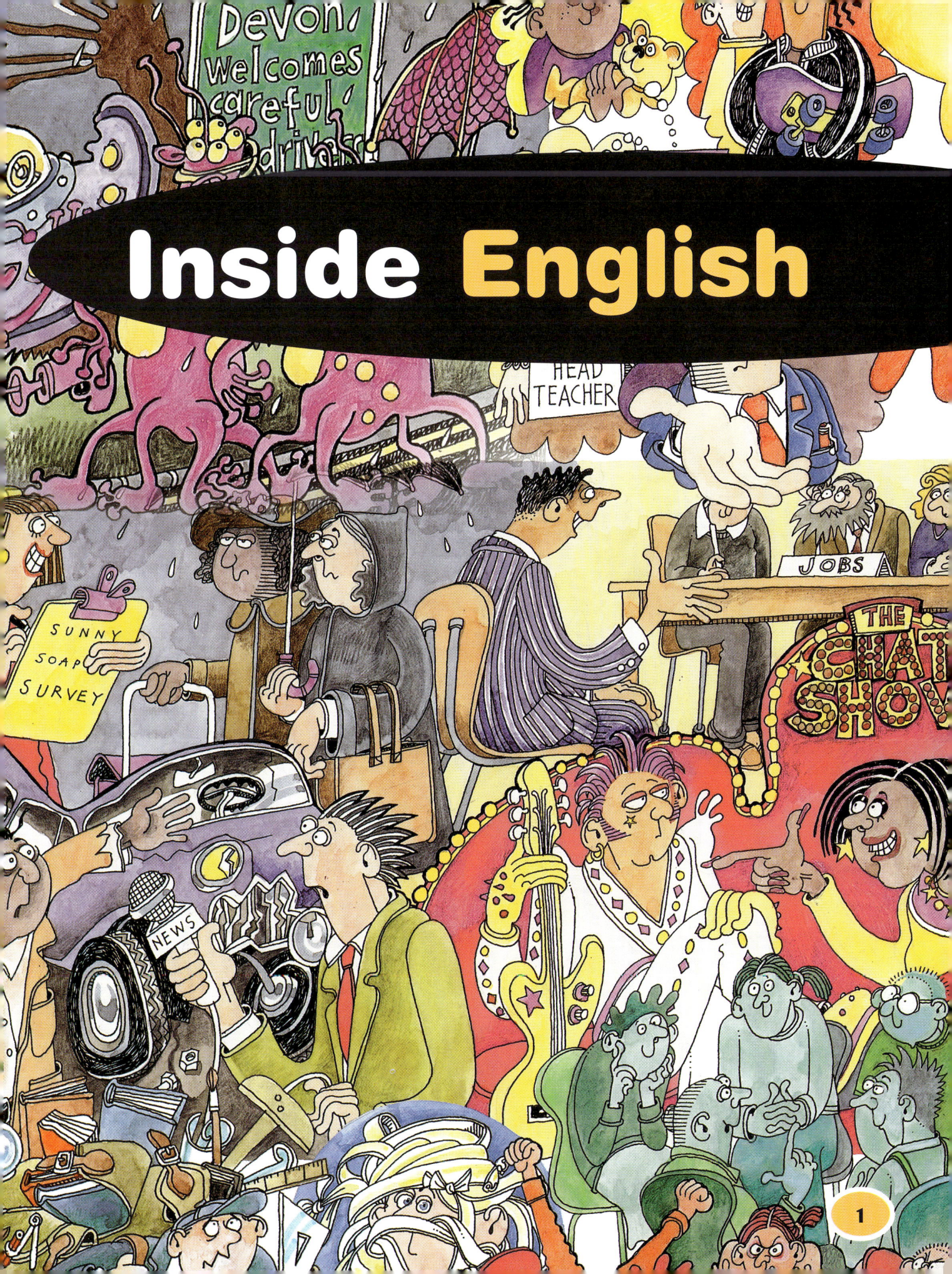

Accent and Dialect

These pages explain the differences between accent, dialect and idiom, and how these relate to standard English.

Accent and dialect are both to do with how people speak, but they mean different things.

Accent

Accent refers to two things:

- **pronunciation** – for example the word *pass* might be pronounced to rhyme with *mass* in the north of England and *farce* in the south
- **intonation** – the musical rise and fall of the speaker's voice.

A **regional** accent is one from a particular area. Do you or people you know have a regional accent? What makes it different from others?

Dialect

Dialect refers to a form of speech found in one area. It includes two things:

- **vocabulary** – individual words, such as *thrang* (Scots, 'full') and *grockle* (West country, 'tourist')
- **grammar** – differences in the way sentences are put together, especially word order, and how verbs are used with nouns or pronouns (see pages 22–23).

The word idiom refers to whole phrases or sayings used in one area. Examples are:

He was fit to be tied
(Northern Ireland, 'He was very angry').

Well, I'll go to the foot of our stairs!
(West Midlands, 'I'm amazed!').

He couldny tackle a fish supper
(Glasgow, said of a poor footballer).

Some examples of grammar differences are:

Sorry it is that you'll be (Irish, 'You'll be sorry').
You eat? (Creole, 'Have you eaten?').
She were late (Yorkshire, 'She was late').

About Spoken English

Standard English

Standard English is the most widely understood form of English. It is used by newsreaders, and anyone who needs to be understood by as many people as possible. Accents and dialects make English more interesting. However, you need to be able to speak standard English when you might otherwise be misunderstood. You can speak it with any accent. The poem below includes both accent and dialect.

Sir Patrick Spens

The king sits in Dunfermline town,
Drinking the blude-red wine;
'O whar will I get a skeely skipper
To sail this new ship o' mine?'

Up and spak an eldern knight,
Sat at the king's right knee:
'Sir Patrick Spens is the best sailor
That ever sail'd the sea.

Our king has written a braid letter,
And seal'd it wi' his hand,
And sent it to Sir Patrick Spens,
Was walking on the strand.

To Noroway, to Noroway,
To Noroway o'er the faem;
The king's daughter o' Noroway,
'Tis thou maun bring her hame.'

(**Anon**.)

summary
- Accent refers to pronunciation and the intonation (rise and fall) of a voice.
- Dialect refers to regional differences in vocabulary and grammar.
- Idiom refers to whole phrases or sayings found especially in one area.
- Standard English is the most widely understood form of English.

Questions

1. In what two ways do regional accents differ from each other?
2. In what two ways are dialects different from standard English?
3. What is an idiom?
4. When should you use standard English, and why?
5. You can't speak standard English with a regional accent. True or false?

1. List the sentences spoken in the picture. Beside each, write what you think it means. Here are standard English versions of the more difficult phrases: 'What are you playing at?'; 'I'm just mending ...'; 'You can't have ...'.
2. Read the poem aloud in a Scottish accent. Write it out in standard English. Use the following words to replace dialect words in the poem: skilful; plain; beach; foam; must. You can work out where to use them by the sense.
3. List the words in the poem that are not dialect but which suggest a Scottish accent. Add their normal spellings. The first is in the second line.
4. Write a dialogue (conversation) between two friends meeting on the street. They can speak in the same dialect, or in different dialects. Begin with greetings and end with goodbyes. Start each speech on a new line, with the speaker's name.

1. Make a dialect dictionary or phrasebook for your area. It may help to ask an elderly neighbour or relative for words and phrases to include.
2. Watch at least three television soaps — but not all in one evening! Make a table showing the programme name, the accents or dialects characters use, and what makes these styles of speech recognisable.

For more information on standard English spelling see pages 12–13

Informal and Formal Register

intro

The style of speech suited to a particular situation is called the **register**. This is not connected to what your teacher calls first thing in the morning! The register varies according to **who** we are speaking to, **why** we are speaking, and **what** we are speaking about.

These pages explain how effective speakers change their style of speech to suit different situations.

Audience **Purpose** **Subject**

Formal and informal

An important point in deciding what register to use is how formal or informal you feel you need to be.

About Spoken English

Getting the wrong register

The people here haven't quite got it right.

> - Good speakers alter their style according to **who** they are speaking to, **why** they are speaking, and **what** they are speaking about.
> - The result of this alteration is the register.
> - What register you use depends partly on how formal you need to be.

summary

Questions

1. What three things should influence your choice of register?
2. Name three formal situations and three informal ones.
3. Write out simple but more formal versions of the following: 'Hang on a sec'; 'I'm gutted!'; 'Got the dosh?'; 'Me and me mates was just 'avin a bit of a laugh'.
4. Write out less formal versions of the following: 'I do not find you attractive'; 'He uses force to make those weaker than himself comply with his wishes'.

1. Draw pictures to show three situations of your own in which someone is speaking in the wrong register.
2. Write down several lines of dialogue (speech) from a novel or story. Leave out any description. Comment on how the characters' style of speech is suited to their situation and their relationship with each other.
3. Watch or listen to the news on television or radio. Note down, and then write out neatly, at least four sentences spoken by the newsreader. Rewrite the lines in the style you might use in speaking to friends.

1. Write a story or picture story in which a character is in a variety of situations and changes register accordingly. Try to include at least three different situations.
2. Write an informal letter to a friend about an awful holiday. Then write a formal letter to the travel agent complaining about it.

For more help with formal and informal letter writing see pages 72–73

5

How Spoken Language Changes

Much-used words gradually change meaning over time, as people use them in slightly different ways. In Shakespeare's time, the word *naughty* was quite insulting, meaning 'worth nothing' (nought). The same is true of *saucy*. To be *amazed* was to be lost in astonishment, not just surprised. Other words change even more. For example, to Shakespeare *ecstasy* meant madness, whereas now it means bliss.

These pages explain how words change their meaning, new words are introduced, and slang comes into fashion and disappears.

New uses

New uses develop mostly through everyday speech. For example, the noun jack-knife (a folding knife) is now used as a verb: 'The lorry jack-knifed on the motorway'.

Some words and phrases with precise professional meanings come to be used more generally. To *drum up* support once referred to army recruiting, but now it has a wider meaning. Another army phrase is *awol*. To 'go awol' is to disappear without telling anyone where you're going. It comes from AWOL meaning Absent Without Leave. Many phrases come from sport, such as *kick-off*, *a level playing field*, and to *score an own-goal*.

Science and medicine

Science and medicine have brought a number of words with Greek and Latin roots into English to name discoveries and inventions, for example television, telephone, hydrogen, pylon.

Technology

New technologies create new expressions. One early one is *hoist with his own petard*, which literally means 'blown up by his own bomb'. Shakespeare uses it for 'caught out by his own trick'. More recently, radio has given us *tune in* and *wavelength*: 'Tune in to my wavelength'. To finish your homework faster you'll need to *shift up a gear* and *go into hyperdrive* – or your teacher might *go ballistic*! What technologies are these phrases from?

Foreign imports

Throughout history, trade and exploration have led to the introduction of many foreign words in English. For example, bandanna (Portuguese, from Hindi), bravado (Spanish), bungalow (Gujerati), curry (Tamil), delicatessen (Dutch/German), depot (French), graffiti (Italian), jungle (Hindi), macho (Spanish), pizza (Italian), pyjamas (Urdu), and thug (Hindi). Do you know of any others?

Slang

Informal words or phrases that are not considered standard English, and are not regional dialect (see pages 2–3), are called **slang**. Slang usually starts as spoken language, and is not often used in print.

Many slang words and phrases are humorous. Some have unexpected meanings, for example, a *Kirby kiss* is a punch in the mouth. Part of the pleasure in using slang lies in knowing what it means, and knowing that not everyone else does.

The Irish writer Jonathan Swift (born in 1667) was worried that if English continued to change so fast, no writer would be understood and appreciated for more than a few years. He wanted an Academy of English to make rules to stop English changing.

About Spoken English

This is also true of rhyming slang. Examples are: rabbit (rabbit and pork – talk); a butcher's (butcher's hook – look); and Adam and Eve (believe).

Speakers also like to think they know the latest slang, so slang words often go out of fashion once most people understand them.

summary

- Over time, words change their meanings through use.
- Some new words and phrases come from professions, some from technology, and some from other languages.
- Slang is informal language, often humorous, and used more in speech than in print.

Questions

1 Name three words that have come from technology.
2 Name three types of technology that have introduced new words and phrases into English.
3 How did *bungalow* and *thug* come into English?
4 Define 'slang' in your own words.

1 List the slang words shown in the picture. Tick those you use or hear used. Add any others that you know. Write definitions for the ones you understand.
2 Make up rhyming slang for the following words: happy; sad; book; bully; steal; shout.
3 Find at least ten slang words or phrases in comics or magazines. List them, with their standard English meanings.

Make an English slang phrasebook for a person of your own age who is visiting Britain and has only learnt standard English.

For more information about where words come from see pages 10–11

7

Differences Between Speech and Writing

intro

Understanding the differences between spoken and written English will help you use both effectively. The table below shows the main differences. What others are there?

> These pages are about the differences between spoken and written English.

The main differences between spoken and written English

Spoken	Written
Usually aimed at one or two people – unless it's a speech.	Usually aimed at a large audience of strangers – except letters and schoolwork.
Speaker present (or on phone). Can use facial expression, hands and tone of voice.	Writer is invisible to reader. Must use words to express everything.
Can be informal and in non-standard English unless in a formal situation (see pages 4–5). Listener can ask questions.	More formal standard English. Must be self-explanatory. Fewer contractions such as *don't*, *it's*.
Heard immediately, but speaker can correct, or explain if not understood.	Writer can redraft and get words exactly right – even in long sentences.
Informal speeches quite short. Longer ones can be divided up by link phrases such as 'Now then ...'.	Can use headings, paragraphs and punctuation. Reader can go slowly and read more than once.

The family scene below shows everyday speech between people who know each other well.
Notice that they speak informally, and not always in standard English or full sentences.
They also rely on knowing a lot about each other. Sam is 11, Julie 13.

Mum: Come on you — it'll get cold.
Sam: I like it cold.
Julie: There's the fridge.
Sam: Not that cold — stupid! Ow! It's too hot. Aaagh — water, water, water!
Julie: Mum...
Sam: Chuck us the sauce.
Mum: Pass.
Julie: Your starter for ten, what is the...
Sam: Shut it you! Where are we goin' on holiday?
Granddad: Blackpool's nice.
Mum: Ooh! Did you remember the form? You know, cos you'll get in trouble.
Sam: Er... I think... 'ang on a sec...
Granddad: Where's me...
Mum: You're wearin' them! Honolulu.
Sam: Honna who-who?
Julie: Where's that? Oh, right, that's where...

8

About Spoken English

Granddad: All grass skirts 'n' that.
Sam: Bahamas?
Granddad: Bananas, coconuts, dates...
Julie: South Pole. I wanna go there. Penguins 'n' polar bears.
Sam: That's north, stupid. Ow!
Granddad: I ate a penguin once.
Mum: Then eat your tea.

A **monologue** is an uninterrupted speech by one person. Read Granddad's, below:

It was in the Falklands. I was in the Specials — Special Combat Group, that was. Oh, and, er...this Welshman — Taffy we called 'im — he tried to get us to say his real name...what was it? Anyway, so Taffy — no, wait a minute, it was this other bloke, Tom — says penguins are dead nutritious 'n' that. Bit salty, bit fishy, you know, but full of goodness.

- Writing is more formal than speech. It is usually aimed at an audience of strangers.
- A speaker can use facial expression, hands and tone. A writer can use headings, paragraphs and punctuation.

summary

Questions

1. When is writing not aimed at an audience of strangers?
2. Which is more informal — speech or writing?
3. How can speech make up for having no punctuation?
4. What can you do if you don't understand a piece of writing straight away?

1. You can either be told how to fit a new brake cable on your bike, or be given written instructions. Explain your choice.
2. The family scene above is to be shown on television. Choose six lines that would need directions telling the actors how to speak and behave.

Write out the lines, with the directions.
Example:
Julie: [impatiently, pointing to fridge] There's the fridge.

3. Here is part of the family scene, adapted to make it easier to follow on radio. See what changes have been made. Then finish the new version.

Mum: Come on you. Your dinner'll get cold.
Sam: I like it cold.
Julie: Put it in the fridge then.
Sam: I don't like it that cold — stupid! Ow! Mum, she bit me! It's too hot. I need some water!
Julie: Mum — where are we going on holiday?

4. Write Granddad's monologue as he might write it — with professional help — in his life story.

1. Write a typical mealtime scene in your own home. You could rely on memory and imagination, or record a real scene — with your family's permission — and adapt it.
2. Ask an older person to tell you about something interesting or entertaining that happened to him or her. Record it or make notes. Write it in your own words as part of the person's life story.

9

English Word Roots

English words are spoken, written and understood by millions of people around the world. Most people never think about where all those words came from in the first place, or about how English has changed and developed as it has spread across the world. As you learn about the **origins** of English, and its many changes, you will also look at the **roots** of modern words. Taking an interest in word roots can help you to spell more accurately!

> These pages are about the changes that have made the English language what it is today, and how the history of the language helps explain some difficulties with English spelling.

Celts

For nearly a thousand years (500BC to AD500), the people who lived in Britain spoke Celtic, a very different language from English. Celtic words remaining in English today are mainly found in place names. Look at a map of Britain, especially of Wales or Cornwall. Can you find any of these? Here are some examples:

- pen – the top of somewhere
- tor or crag – rocky peak
- combe or cwm – valley
- brock – badger.

Romans

The Romans invaded Britain in AD43 and stayed for over 350 years. Some of the words they used can still be found in place names in many parts of England. For example:

- chester, cester and caster – from the Latin word *castra* meaning army camp
- street – the Latin words *via strata* mean a road that is paved (the Romans built many of these)
- *magna* (big) and *parva* (small) are sometimes attached to place names.

Angles, Saxons and Jutes

These tribes came to Britain from the area of Europe we now call Germany, beginning in about AD450. The language they brought with them is the main root of today's English, though you would probably not recognise it as the same language. It is called **Old English** or **Anglo-Saxon**. Less than a thousand modern English words have Anglo-Saxon roots, but they are the words we use most frequently, for example, *be*, *and*, *house*, *man*, *dog*, *build*, *wife*.

Here are some examples of Anglo-Saxon place names:

- ham – a dwelling or home
- stead or ton – a site settled by people (farmbuildings, or town)
- burgh, bury or borough – a fortified (walled) town or castle
- ford – a river crossing.

Roman missionaries

Around AD600, Christianity was brought to Britain, along with many Latin words linked with religion, such as *shrine*, *school*, *priest*, *abbot*, *cell*, *idol*, *altar* and *martyr*.

Vikings

Scandinavian invaders, whose language was Norse, attacked the north and east of England around AD800. Some Vikings settled, and you can see in which areas of England because of place names ending in:

- by – farm or town, like stead and ton
- thorp or thorpe – village
- thwaite – a lonely place
- kirk – church
- beck – stream.

Spelling

Normans

In 1066 the Normans conquered England. This greatly changed the English language because the Normans introduced new words to describe their way of life, not just place names. Examples include: *mansion, court, castle, prison, prince, baron, judge, jury, money, pork, beef, mutton, feast, salmon, sausage, art, beauty, painting, sculpture, cushion, flower, spaniel, terrier, nice, please, gay, joy.*

The Renaissance

During the Renaissance well-educated people all learned Latin and Greek. To make the English they used different from the spoken English of the people who worked in the fields, they borrowed more words from Latin and Greek.

This difference between words with Anglo-Saxon roots and words with Greek or Latin roots still affects the **vocabulary** of spoken (**colloquial**) and written (**formal**) English to this day. More words with Latin roots include: *inferior, debt, doubt, oriental, scripture, picture, polite, receipt, intellect, ascend, regal.*

Trade, travel and invention

Since that time, British explorers and traders have travelled the world. Everywhere they have been, they have borrowed words for clothing, animals, transport, food and drink, for example:

- Italy — *balcony, confetti, opera, grafitti*
- Middle East — *coffee, caravan, bazaar, kiosk*
- India — *pyjamas, shampoo, ginger, bungalow*
- American-Indian (and Inuit): *moccasin, moose, anorak, igloo*
- Spanish — *cannibal, sherry, potato, cafeteria.*

Science and medicine have brought a number of words with Greek and Latin roots into English to name new discoveries and inventions, such as *pylon, hydrogen, psychiatrist, telephone.*

> - Modern English vocabulary has its roots in many other languages including: Old English, Latin, Norse and French.

summary

Questions

1. Give four different reasons why words from other languages have been added to English vocabulary.
2. Which languages have had the most widespread influence on English place names?
3. What can you guess about the Norman way of life, judging from the words they added to English?
4. Why is there a link between words with Latin roots and formal English?

1. Look at a map of Britain. List examples of each of the following: place names with Latin roots; Celtic roots; Anglo-Saxon roots; Viking roots. Which of these peoples might have lived in your own area, judging from local place names?
2. Draw, or trace, a map of the world. Label it with at least 30 'English' words using arrows to point at the country they came from originally. You can start with these pages, but then find an **etymological dictionary** (one that gives information about word origins), or ask around, to see how many new examples you can collect.
3. These words share the same letters at the beginning, but they sound different. Which root language is linked to which sound? *Chaos, chauffeur, chemist, cheese, chef, charm, chauvinist, charisma, child.*
A good dictionary which explains where words come from will help you to work this out.

Carry out some research into the roots of first names and family names (surnames) used in Britain. Start off with the people in your English class. Find out what their names mean and what language they originally came from.

For more help with word roots see pages 6–7, 16–17 and 18–19

11

Spelling Rules

English is a difficult language to spell because there are so many different ways to say sounds in letters. Even so, there are some rules that are worth putting in the effort to understand and remember, because they work for a large number of English words. Six of these rules are explained here. Learning these rules will help you to sort out common mistakes in spelling.

These pages are about some of the rules which help you to work out how to spell many common English words correctly.

Rule 1: the magic 'e'

The five letters most often used to write the **vowel sounds** (a, e, i, o, u) in English words all have a short sound (how you were taught to say letter sounds when you first learnt to read) and a long sound (the adult alphabet name for the letter).

Adding an 'e' to the end of five short words will show you the different vowel sounds – and it will show you the powerful effect of the magic 'e'.

Short vowel sound	Long vowel sound
hat	hate
pet	Pete
pin	pine
hop	hope
cut	cute

The letter 'i' has the same effect on these five vowel sounds. Once you know this, you will understand the reason for the next two rules.

Rule 2: doubling

The only way you can stop the magic 'e' (or 'i') from changing the sound of these vowels is to double the **consonant** (a letter other than a vowel or 'y') written after the vowel.

So, when you want to make **verb stems** (see page 26) into **present** or **past participles** (by adding -ing or -ed), to keep a short vowel sound, you must double the consonant. Here are some examples of words often spelled wrongly:

Verb stem	-ing	-ed
tap	tapping	tapped
label	labelling	labelled
stop	stopping	stopped

Rule 3: dropping the 'e' or not?

When you add -ing or -ed to words with a long vowel sound, you can drop the 'e' from the stem, because these endings make the vowel sound long anyway (but remember not to double any consonants).

Verb stem	-ing	-ed
tape	taping	taped
dine	dining	dined
poke	poking	poked

Rule 4: 'i before e'

Learn the following rhyme – and you will know how to spell most words with 'ie' or 'ei' in the middle:

When the sound is 'ee'
As in 'meet'
It's i before e
Except after c

Here are some examples of 'ie' words: *thief, believe, brief, chief, field*. (Note: 'after c' does not mean 'after ch' – that is a different sound.)

These are some 'after c' words: *receive, ceiling, deceive, conceited* – and some rule breakers (nothing is simple with English spelling!): *weird, seize*.

Spelling

Rule 5: adding 's' to noun plurals and verbs

We add 's' to the ends of words for two main reasons:

- It shows the word is a **plural** – that there is more than one thing, for example *two footballs*.
- It shows that a word is a **third person present tense**, for example *he waits, she chooses*.

If the **noun** or verb stem already ends in 's', 'ch', 'sh', 'x' or 'z', you have to add 'es', to reflect the way the word is said, for example: *some churches, three wishes, he boxes well, the bee buzzes*.

If the noun or verb ends in 'y', after a vowel add 's' as normal. But if the 'y' is after a consonant, change the 'y' to 'i' and then add 'es'. Compare: *the boys, he plays*, with *the babies, she flies*.

If the noun or verb ends in 'o' after a vowel, just add 's' as normal, but if the word ends in 'o' after a consonant, add 'es'. Compare: *the recording studios, he radios for help*, with *a pound of tomatoes, it echoes*.

If the noun ends with 'f' or 'fe', change the 'f' to 'v' and add 'es' or 's'. So, *a life* becomes *nine lives*, and *a thief* becomes *40 thieves*. (Some words that do not follow the rule: *roofs* and *chiefs*.)

Rule 6: -ly endings on adverbs

When you turn an **adjective** into an **adverb** (see page 24) by adding -ly, it hardly ever changes the spelling of the adjective. No final 'e' is dropped, no letters are doubled, and the -ly ending does not suddenly grow an 'e' in its middle. Here are some commonly misspelled adverbs: *definite-ly, separate-ly, hopeful-ly, lone-ly*.

summary

- Rule 1: final 'e' makes vowel sounds 'long'.
- Rule 2: doubled letters make vowel sounds 'short'.
- Rule 3: drop the 'e' when adding -ing or -ed to words with long vowel sounds.
- Rule 4: 'i before e except after c'.
- Rule 5: explains how adding 's' to plural noun and third person verbs affects spelling.
- Rule 6: explains how to get correct spellings when adding the ending -ly.

Questions

1. How does the magic 'e' change vowel sounds? Which other letter has the same effect?
2. What effect does a double consonant have when written after a vowel sound?
3. What is the complete rhyme which reminds you whether a word is spelt with 'ie' or 'ei'?
4. Explain two purposes for adding 's' or 'es' to the end of a word.

1. Use the magic 'e' and doubling rules to make sure the spelling of the verb and participle in brackets is correct. Vowel sounds should be kept long or short, as they started off:

   a) I was hope (ing) to win the hop (ing) race.
   b) I was begin (ing) to like swim (ing) very much.
   c) I was run (ing) to the dine (ing) room to be on time for the carve (ing) of the meat.

2. Follow the rules and add 's' to these nouns and verbs:

   a) The baby(s) like their new toy (s).
   b) The lady(s) cut the loaf(s) into half(s) with sharp knife(s).
   c) The sound of the donkey(s') hoof(s) echo(s) down the lane.

3. Fred and Freda like writing stories, but they are terrible at spelling. This is their latest effort. Write down their 20 mistakes and correct them. Then explain at least two rules from these pages you think Fred and Freda really need to learn.

   The Mysterys of the Old Archs
   It is barley dark but already John is swiming silentley across the lake. He beleives that this will definetley be the night the theifs will recieve thier just deserts. They have robed The Archs, where John's two old auntys live, three times. Just as John is begining to shiver with the cold, he spys something moveing in the bushs. He siezes the branchs above his head and crashs on to dry land.

If you know you have a problem with spelling one or more of the groups of words covered by these rules, write down all the examples on these pages in your spelling notebook. (Make sure you write the words with their correct spelling!)

For more information on spelling see pages 10–11, 14–15, 16–17 and 18–19

Better Spelling

intro

It is not easy to become an excellent speller of English. Different people have different problems and find different ways to overcome them. You will have to make up your own mind about the best way for you to become a better speller. Below are seven ideas to help you.

> These pages are about different ways to help you remember the correct spelling of tricky words.

1 Spelling notebook

Make your own spelling lists. You could do this in a small notebook, or you could make a list on a computer.

If you use a notebook, put the letters of the alphabet at the top of the page, and organise your word lists like a mini-dictionary. On a computer, you can type in words you want to learn and let the computer sort them into alphabetical order.

Once you have made your notebook, use it for four things:

- List spelling corrections from your school books.
- Collect new words you learn in school, or from your reading.
- Check the correct spelling of any problem words when you are writing.
- Learn your problem words by reading them over regularly and asking someone to test you when you think you know five words.

2 Look, cover, write, check

Use your eyes to remember what words look like. When you write a word into your spelling notebook, or find a word in the dictionary to use in your writing, do the following:

- Look at the word carefully and fix the pattern of the letters into your memory.
- Cover the word up, so you cannot see it.
- Write the word from memory – look at the pattern of letters carefully to see if it looks right.
- Check your spelling of the word with the correct spelling in your notebook or dictionary. Correct it if you made a mistake. Look carefully at the correct spelling.

3 Letter patterns

If you are not very good at remembering things just by looking at them, try this. The words in the table below all share letter patterns which are often found in English spelling. Of course, they are not always pronounced the same way! Let your hand learn the pattern. Look for the letter pattern in the groups of words and then write (or type) that group of letters once with your eyes open, then twice with your eyes closed.

4 Sounding

Some people remember things they hear better than things they see. Try this and see if it helps you. Break up long, hard words into **syllables** (see page 18), and say the sounds of each little bit out loud each time you write the word, emphasising the vowel sound. Here are some examples:

nec-es-sar-y
def-in-ite-ly
se-pa-rate-ly

where	there	here	nowhere	therefore	heredity
national	stationary	foundation	sensational	circulation	recreation
favourite	resource	humour	floury	hour	tourist

Spelling

5 Memory tricks

Pairs of words which sound the same but have different spellings can be a problem. You need to find some simple trick to jog your memory. For example, remember that the word 'stationery' (writing equipment) has the letter 'e' for envelope in it. Then you won't mix it up with 'stationary' (standing still).

'*Practice*' (a noun) is spelled differently from '*practise*' (a verb). Remember that '*advice*' (noun) and '*advise*' (verb) follow the same spelling pattern, but they sound different. Other words that follow this rule include *licence/license* and *prophecy/prophesy*.

6 Mnemonics

Make up a short, funny saying using the letters of a problem spelling – a mnemonic. For example, you could remember how to spell '*meant*' by the mnemonic 'monster eggs are never tasty'. To remember '*said*': 'soggy aliens invade Devon'.

7 Words inside words

Sometimes it will help you to remember the spelling of a long difficult word if you look for short words inside it. Can you spot any words inside these long words: *reputable, potatoes, foreigner, hypothesis, mathematics*?

The seven different ways to remember how to spell a tricky word:
- Write it in your spelling notebook.
- Learn the movement of any letter patterns.
- Make up a trick to jog your memory.
- Look for words inside the word.
- Look, cover, write, check it.
- Sound it out in syllables.
- Make up a mnemonic.

summary

Questions

1. Name an advantage of keeping a spelling list on your computer.
2. Make up a memory trick to remind you that *accommodation* has two 'c's and two 'm's.
3. Make up mnemonics for the tricky letter sequence 'ould' in *could, would, should*.
4. Copy out the following words: *pleasure, secretary, important, disobedient*. Underline any short words you spot inside them.

1. Make a spelling notebook. Start your lists of tricky words by writing down any ten words on these pages which would cause you a spelling problem. Make sure you use the look, cover, write, check technique.
2. Which three words cause you the biggest spelling problems? Invent mnemonics for each one.
3. The author George Bernard Shaw made up the word 'ghoti' to show how difficult it is to learn English spelling. It says 'fish', using 'f' from cou**gh**, 'i' from w**o**men and 'sh' from sta**ti**on. Make up five crazy spellings of your own – and see if your family or friends can work out what the words are. Suggestions for fun words to try: *Friday, coffee, shampoo, terrify, rifle*.

Collect ten long, difficult words of your own choice and look for 'words inside words'.

For more information on spelling see pages 10–11, 12–13, 16–17 and 18–19

Using a Dictionary and Thesaurus

intro

A **dictionary** will help you to spell more accurately, as well as giving you other information about the words you look up. A **thesaurus** will help you to develop and make use of many more words, improving your **vocabulary**.

These pages are about ways to improve your spelling and choice of words by showing you how to make the best use of a dictionary and a thesaurus.

What can you find out from a dictionary?

A dictionary can help you improve your spelling. It will also tell you a lot more about each word, once you know how to decode the information you are given.

The shortest, simplest dictionary will tell you:

① how to spell the word
② how to say it – its **pronunciation** – if this is not clear from the spelling
③ whether it is a **noun**, **verb**, **adverb** or other **part of speech** (see pages 20–26).
④ what it means – the **definition**
⑤ other words connected with the main word.

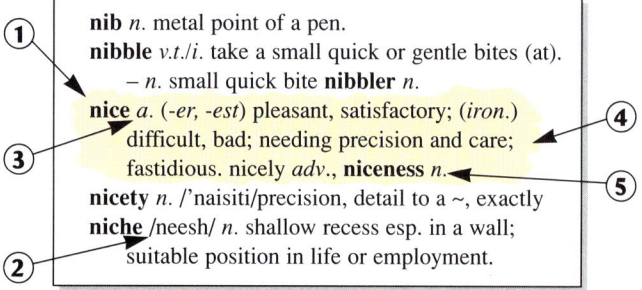

from *The Oxford Mini Dictionary* by Joyce M Hawkins

Larger dictionaries give extra information about the origins (root) of the word and examples of the word in use, possibly showing how it has changed over time. Dictionaries which explain the **derivations** (origins) of words are called **etymological** dictionaries.

Using a dictionary

All dictionaries list words in alphabetical order. You would find these fruits listed in this order:
apple, banana, lemon, melon, pineapple.

If the first letter of the words is the same, the second letter is the one which decides the order of the list:
pear, pineapple, plum, pumpkin.

If the first and second letters are the same, then the order of words depends on the third letter, and so on:
pea, peach, peanut, pear.

To help you find the right page quickly, at the top of each page there are two words. On the left-hand side is the first word listed on the page. On the right-hand side is the last word listed.

At the front of the dictionary, there will be a page (or even several pages) to explain the codes the dictionary uses to cram all the information it gives into a small space. These codes will include symbols used:

- to show how words are pronounced, for example, 'k shows the hard c sound'
- to show the different parts of speech, for example, 'n'. means noun
- to show different language roots, for example, 'G' means Greek
- to show how a word is used, for example, 'sl. slang'.

Using a thesaurus

This word has its roots in a Greek word that means a treasury or a store-house. Learning how to use a thesaurus will do more than help you to spell: it will give you access to a much larger vocabulary than you would normally use.

Spelling

The simplest kind of thesaurus is organised like a dictionary – words are listed in alphabetical order. The information in a thesaurus is very different. Instead of a definition, it gives you a list of **synonyms** (other words with a similar meaning) of the main word.

The children's thesaurus below shows you:

1. the main word
2. the part of speech
3. synonyms for two different meanings of the main word
4. opposites (**antonyms**) of the two different meanings.

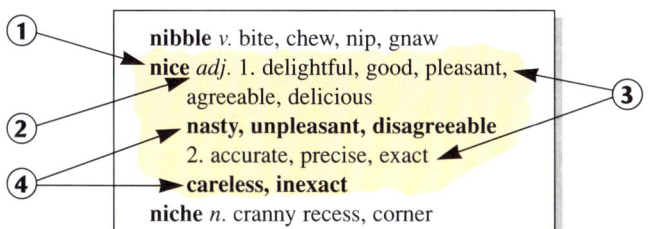

nibble *v.* bite, chew, nip, gnaw
nice *adj.* 1. delightful, good, pleasant, agreeable, delicious
nasty, unpleasant, disagreeable
2. accurate, precise, exact
careless, inexact
niche *n.* cranny recess, corner

from *The Kingfisher Illustrated Thesaurus* by John Bellamy

Using *Roget's Thesaurus*

Roget's Thesaurus is the original thesaurus. It may be the one you find in the library, or at home. To use this, you need to get used to a different way of listing words.

At the back of the book is an **index** where words are listed in alphabetical order, like a dictionary. It is possible that the index might give you a suitable alternative word.

> **nice** *pleasant* 376 adj.
> *savoury* 390 adj.
> *careful* 457 adj.
> *discriminating* 463 adj.

If you wish to look for a wider selection of words, look up the number given after the word. This is not a page number, but the number of a list of synonyms. These lists are arranged in groups of words connected to a particular topic at the front of the book.

summary

- Any dictionary gives you this information about each main word: correct spelling, part of speech, definition, other words connected to the main word.
- Some dictionaries also give you information about: pronunciation, word roots, examples of how the word is used.
- Any thesaurus will give you information about words with a similar meaning to the main word.

Questions

A

1. Put these words into alphabetical order: *freckle, forgive, friend, freak, frantic, fox, frank, foul.*
2. Which three of the above words would not be on the dictionary page with the words *fowl* and *free* printed at the top?
3. What part of speech is the word *nice*?
4. Which different meanings can the word *nice* have?
5. Suggest two synonyms for *nice* and two antonyms taken from the thesaurus entries on these pages.

B

1. Rewrite the postcard message below, using the thesaurus entries on these pages to replace the repeated words:

   Having a nice time here. Weather is nice, and we're staying in a very nice hotel with a nice view. Went to a nice restaurant last night, Sarah wore that nice dress you chose. Our meal was really nice, too. Hope the horrid weather at home is improving. It will be nice to see you when we get home, but horrid to have to go back to school.

2. Choose four words from your local dialect, or the slang expressions you hear in school. Write dictionary definitions for each word giving as much information as you can about: part of speech, pronunciation and examples of use.
3. Write an explanation of how to find information about word derivations in an etymological dictionary and how to use *Roget's Thesaurus*. If possible, find your own examples to illustrate your description. Try the words *malice* in the dictionary and *bad* in the thesaurus.

C

Look up the following words in a thesaurus and collect at least five synonyms for each: *big, small, hard, soft, very, many, get, get back, get better, get up.*

For more information on spelling see pages 10–11 and 18–19
For more information on spelling rules see pages 12–13

Sounds and Syllables

intro

Words have a grammar of their own. You can take a word apart to see how it works just as you can take a sentence apart. The smallest parts of a spoken word are its **sounds** and these combine into **syllables**. The smallest parts of a written word are its **letters**. Paying attention to the parts that make up words and recognising patterns is another way of improving your spelling skills.

> These pages are about how words are put together from smaller parts called syllables, compound words, prefixes and suffixes.

Sounds and letters: consonants and vowels

In spoken English, you will be able to hear about 44 different sounds. Around 20 of these are **vowel** sounds, the others are **consonants**. When we write English, we only have 26 letters for all those different sounds. The five letters 'a, e, i, o, u' and sometimes 'y' are all used to write vowel sounds, either on their own or together. The other letters are all used, on their own or together, to write consonant sounds.

Syllables

A **syllable** is a part of a word that only has one vowel sound (though it may have more than one vowel letter) in it. The word *to-day* has two syllables; *to-morr-ow* has three syllables; *dic-tion-ar-y* has four syllables.

Compound words

Compound words are words made by joining together two (or more) simpler words. Sometimes the meaning of the compound word is the same as its parts, sometimes it is not so obvious. For example, a *greenhouse* is not the same thing as a *green house*. Here are some other examples: *saucepan, air-condition, textbook, blackboard, supermarket, hairdresser, takeaway, scapegoat, bloodthirsty, dog-eared*.

Prefixes

Prefixes are attached to the beginnings of words. They change the meaning of the word they are added to – the **base word** – in the following ways:

- *fore-* means in front or before
  (*forecourt, forefront, forethought, forewarn*)
- *mis-* means wrongly
  (*miscount, mislead, misprint, misshape*)
- *pre-* means before
  (*prearrange, predial, pre-exist, prepay*)
- *un-* means not
  (*unkind, ungrateful, unlikely, unwrap*).

Suffixes

Suffixes are attached to the ends of words. They can do different jobs. Some suffixes change the **word class** of the **base word**. For example, *-ful* makes nouns into adjectives – *hate* becomes *hateful*, *pity* becomes *pitiful*, and so on. The suffix *-ty* changes adjectives into nouns, so that *cruel* becomes *cruelty*, etc.

> Some compound words and words beginning with a prefix may be linked by a hyphen, for example, *co-pilot, hot-tub*. Some words can be spelt either with or without the hyphen. When in doubt, check in the dictionary.

Spelling

Some suffixes change verb tenses or make nouns plural, but do not alter word class:

- *-ed* is the most common past tense suffix, for example, *melted*.
- *-s* is the most common suffix to make nouns plural, for example, *flowers*.

Some suffixes adapt the meaning of the words they attach to. For example, these suffixes show something is small: *-ling* (*duckling*), *-let* (*booklet*), *-ock* (*hillock*), *-kin* (*mannikin*). This suffix shows something is female: *-ess* (*actress, countess, princess*).

Some of the longest words in English are put together with many prefixes and suffixes. Here is an example: *antidisestablishmentarianism*. What is the base word? How many prefixes and suffixes are attached to it? Look up its meaning in a good dictionary.

Classical prefixes and suffixes

Many English words are put together from prefixes and suffixes which have Greek or Latin origins. You will see that some of these can be used both at beginnings and ends of words.

- *tele-* means from a distance (*television, telephone, telescope*)
- *anti-* means against (*anticlockwise, antiperspirant*)
- *ante-* means before (*antedate, antenatal*)
- *bio-* means life (*biology, biography*)
- *auto-* means self (*autobiography, automobile*)
- *photo-* means light (*photoelectric, photosynthesis*)
- *-logy* means knowledge about (*biology, geology*)
- *-graphy* means writing or drawing (*biography, photography*)
- *-phile* means a lover of something (*Anglophile, philosopher*)
- *-phobia* means a fear of something (*claustrophobia, arachnophobia*)
- *-anthropy* means people or humankind (*philanthropy, anthropologist*)

- The smallest parts of a spoken word are its sounds. These divide into vowels and consonants.
- A syllable is a part of a word with just one vowel sound.
- A compound word is made up of several smaller words.
- Prefixes attach to beginnings of words. Suffixes attach to the ends of words

summary

Questions

1. How many letters in the English alphabet are used to write vowel sounds?
2. How many letters are used to write consonant sounds?
3. What is a compound word? Give three examples.
4. What is a prefix? What is a suffix?

1. The suffixes *-ary, -eer, -ior, -ist* and *-wright* are all used to show people's interests, skills or jobs. Write down as many examples as you can of words ending with each one.
2. Write down as many words as you can which include any of prefixes and suffixes taken from Latin and Greek listed here.

Make a collection of compound words. Try to identify all the different parts of speech they can be made from. For example, *blackbird* is noun + noun, *bloodthirsty* is noun + adjective, *red-hot* is adjective + adjective, *waterlogged* is noun + verb.

For more information on word roots see pages 10–11

Nouns, Articles and Adjectives

Nouns and **adjectives** are the parts of speech we use to name and describe things we see in the world around us.

These pages are about different kinds of nouns and adjectives.

What do nouns do?
Here is a well-known nursery rhyme but with every noun missed out. What does it tell you about the information nouns give in a sentence?

_____ and _____ went up the _____
To fetch a _____ of _____,
_____ fell down and broke his _____,
And _____ came tumbling after.

Nouns are names. A noun can be the name of a person, a place, an object, an animal, a group or an idea.

Four different kinds of noun
Proper noun – the name of a particular person, place or thing. It begins with a capital letter, for example, *Jill, Glasgow, Thursday, Nintendo*.

Common noun – the name shared by people, things, places of the same type. It is called this because the name is common to a lot of things of the same kind, for example, *hill, pail, boy, computer game*.

Collective noun – the name given to a group of people or things, such as *team, family, herd, army*.

Abstract noun – the name given to an idea or a feeling. It is called this because you cannot see, hear or touch these things, for example, *kindness, cruelty, boredom, fear*.

What is an article?
Words such as '*a*' or '*the*' often appear before a common noun or collective noun, when these words are in a sentence. These are **articles**. Other words used as articles include '*an*' and '*some*'.

'*The*' is called the **definite article**. It shows that the noun refers to one specific item. '*A*' or '*an*' is called the **indefinite article** because the noun could refer to any one of a number of similar items. What difference does the article make in the following sentences?

Lend me a pencil.
Lend me the pencil.

What do adjectives do?
Adjectives give you more information about nouns. They are words which help describe people, places, things or ideas. There are five different kinds of adjective.

- **Adjectives of quality** tell you what sort of thing it is, for example, a *steep, green, grassy hill*.
- **Interrogative adjectives** ask questions, such as: *Which* boy fell down? *Whose* head was hurt?
- **Possessive adjectives** show ownership, for example, Jack hurt *his* head, Jack and Jill dropped *their* pail.
- **Adjectives of quantity** tell you how many things there are, for example, *three* pencils, *some* water.
- **Deictic adjectives** point out specific things, such as: *that* boy, *these* girls.

Comparatives and superlatives
Adjectives of quality have three forms which we may use when we want to make comparisons.

This is a steep hill. **Steep** is the ordinary adjective we use to describe one thing.

That is a steeper hill than this one. **Steeper** is a **comparative** adjective, used to compare two things.

Over there is the steepest hill of all the ones round here. **Steepest** is a **superlative** adjective, used to compare three or more things.

Grammar

There are two very common adjectives that change completely to make comparative and superlative forms. You need to remember these are different:

good better best
bad worse worst

Instead of using *-er* and *-est* endings, you can say:

That hill is more steep than this. (Comparative)
That is the most steep hill round here. (Superlative)

For some adjectives, this is the only way to make comparatives and superlatives. Examples include *beautiful, industrious, magnificent* and many other adjectives with the same endings (*-ful, -ious* and *-ent*). But remember that you never need both.

Words which show how much

More and *most* are examples of **adverbs of degree**. Usually adverbs tell you more about verbs, but this type is different. These words can qualify adjectives to tell you about their extent or degree. They answer the question: how much does the adjective apply to the noun? For example:

Jack tied a *remarkably* untidy bandage on his head.

Jill told him bandages which are *too* tight can be *very* dangerous.

summary

- Nouns are names. There are four types of these: proper, common, collective, abstract.
- Articles introduce nouns. There are two types: definite and indefinite. Articles are a type of adjective.
- Adjectives give more information about nouns. There are five types: quality, quantity, interrogative, possessive, deictic. Comparative adjectives compare two things; superlative adjectives compare three or more things.
- Adverbs of degree can qualify adjectives and adverbs.

Questions

1. Write down two proper nouns, two common nouns and two abstract nouns. How do the things abstract nouns name differ from the other things on your list?
2. What collective nouns would you use to describe a group or collection of each of these: goats, seagulls, football fans?
3. List four adjectives which do not form comparatives and superlatives by adding *-er* and *-est*.
5. What is an adverb of degree?

1. List the words in bold. Write down for each one 'article' or 'adjective'.

Then write which kind of adjective they are.

Five birds perched on **my** fence. From **the next** garden came **a** noise. **Most** birds would fly away, but **these** ones didn't. **My** cat licked **its** lips.

2. What is wrong with these comparisons? Spot, and correct, the grammatical slips.

He's the fastest of the pair of them.
I'm more better at that than you.
It's the baddest place I know.
It's obviouser than you think.
She is the beautifulest supermodel.

3. Point out the five adverbs of degree in the postcard message below. Decide which ones could be missed out without the meaning changing. Write down your improved message.

Having a tremendously enjoyable holiday. Weather fabulously lovely, though midday can be too hot for me. The restaurants are rather expensive, but the food is incredibly delicious.

Redraft a poem or a story you wrote earlier this year. Add two or three adjectives to each noun. Use a thesaurus to find more unusual adjectives than nice, good, bad, big, small, red, blue, etc. Find more unusual alternatives. Then take out the extra words that don't work. Is the result an improvement?

For more information on parts of speech see pages 22–23 and 24–25

21

Pronouns and Noun Phrases

intro

When we want to name things, in speech or writing, sometimes we need more detail than a name on its own will provide, or we want to avoid repeating the name. **Pronouns** and **noun phrases** help us to do both of these.

These pages are about how nouns can be expanded into groups of words, named noun phrases, and how pronouns may be used to replace nouns and noun phrases in a sentence.

What are pronouns and why do we need them?

A pronoun is a word you can use instead of any noun or noun phrase. If we did not have pronouns, we would have to keep repeating the nouns over and over again.

Personal pronouns stand for people or things. For the **subject** of the sentence, these are *I, you, he, she, it, we, they*. For the **object**, some of them are different: *me, him, her, us, them*. (Subject and object are explained on page 28.)

Reflexive pronouns refer to a noun or pronoun mentioned earlier in the sentence. These are *myself, yourself, himself, herself, itself, ourselves, yourselves, themselves*.

Possessive pronouns show who owns something. These are *mine, yours, his, hers, its, ours, theirs*. Remember not to add an apostrophe before the 's' in a pronoun.

Relative pronouns do the job of connecting one **clause** in a sentence to another. These include words like *who, whose, which, that, what*, for example, '*Show me what you won*'.

Interrogative pronouns ask questions. These are mainly the same words as relative pronouns, but used in a different way, for example, '*What did you win?*'.

Indefinite pronouns refer to people or things in general, and sometimes give an idea of quantity. These are words like *some, many, several, anything, nobody, none*.

Deictic pronouns point out specific people or things. These are words like *this, that, these*, and *those*.

H

The names of some kinds of pronoun are the same as some of the different kinds of adjectives (see page 20). Even the words are the same. You can tell when they are used as adjectives, because a noun will follow soon afterwards. But if they are pronouns, they will be on their own, because they are there instead of a noun.

Is it 'I' or is it 'Me'?

When we are talking we sometimes say things like '*Me and my mates got the bus to town*'. We know this is not standard English, so we would change it to '*My friends and I ...*' when we write.

This may be right sometimes, but not always. The rule is, for the **subject** of the sentence, you would write ' *... and I*', as in '*My friends and I caught the bus*'.

But, for the **object** of the sentence, write '*... and me*', as in '*The driver told my friends and me to get off the bus. Later, Jane shared her chips with Jo and me*'.

After all, you would not write '*Me caught the bus*' or '*The driver told I to get off the bus*'. And that is the best way to check you have got it right!

22

Grammar

What is a noun phrase?

A noun phrase is a group of words which does the same job as a noun in a sentence. Articles, adjectives and adverbs of degree may be added to a noun to make one kind of noun phrase.

Noun phrases in sentences

A noun phrase can do **all the same jobs** as a noun on its own in a sentence. A single pronoun can replace a whole noun phrase just the same way as it can stand in for a noun.

Article or adjective	Adverb of degree	As many adjectives of quality as you like	Noun
The	extremely	kind, elderly	gentleman
Those	rather	attractive, spiky, red	flowers
Five	very	rude, noisy	schoolkids

summary

- A pronoun can be used to replace any repeated noun or noun phrase. The most common pronouns are personal pronouns – these are different depending whether they do the job of subject or object in a sentence.
- There are six other types of pronoun. Some of these have the same names and similar, or even the same, words as adjectives with a similar use, for example, interrogative, deictic, possessive.
- Noun phrases can be formed in different ways, some simple, and some more complicated. A noun phrase can do all the same jobs as a noun in a sentence.

Questions

1. Why do we need pronouns?
2. Which kind of pronoun is the most common?
3. How many of the other six kinds of pronoun can you name?
4. What parts of speech make up the simplest kind of noun phrase?

1. Is it I or is it me? Follow the advice given in the box above, and fill in the gaps in this story with the right word.

    Normally Shahida, Rani, Jade and _____ are all good friends. Unfortunately, the other day there was a quarrel between Shahida and _____. After that, Rani and _____ fell out with Shahida. Then Shahida stopped talking to Rani and _____. Jade told our tutor about Shahida and _____. Our tutor said Shahida and _____ had to shake hands and make up. Now Shahida and _____ are the best of friends again. Rani and Jade have forgiven Shahida and _____ for causing such a fuss.

2. This is what a story might look like if we did not have pronouns. Make a list of all the nouns and noun phrases that keep being repeated.

    Shane told the other pupils in Shane's class that Shane's English teacher's grammar lessons were more interesting grammar lessons than any of the other English teacher's grammar lessons. Shane says Shane's English teacher makes Shane's English teacher's grammar lessons entertaining. Now all of the class come to Shane's English teacher's grammar lessons and Shane can't get a seat because all the other pupils pack the room where Shane's English teacher's grammar lessons are held.

3. Read this version of the story. Tick the nouns on your list which are still used here, but write down the pronouns next to the nouns they have replaced.

    Shane told the other pupils in his class that his English teacher's grammar lessons were more interesting ones that those of any others. He said she made hers entertaining. Now all of them come to her grammar lessons and he can't get a seat because they pack the room where her grammar lessons are held.

Take a piece of your own writing and have careful look at it. Can you make your noun phrases more interesting? Are you using pronouns enough? Too often? Correctly?

For more information on nouns and adjectives see pages 20–21
For more information on simple sentences see pages 28–29

Verbs, Adverbs and Prepositions

intro

The parts of speech explained below are connected because they give information about where things are and how they move about. But that is just part of what you will discover, so read on to find out about **verbs**, **adverbs** and **prepositions**.

These pages are about what verbs, adverbs and prepositions do in sentences and how to recognise different kinds of verbs and adverbs.

What do verbs do?

One of the easiest ways to see what verbs do in a sentence is to try making sense of writing with all the verbs missed out. What is happening here?

The Security Guard _____ very strong.
He _____ an intruder. The intruder _____ surprised, but still he _____ .
As quickly as possible, he _____ into his get-away car and _____ off down the road.
The Guard _____ pleased that he _____ his job well.

Think of just one word to complete each gap in the story. You will soon see that your version of the story tells you two things about verbs.

A verb has two main purposes in a sentence. It tells you:

- **what is happening**.
  It can tell you an action – what someone **does** – such as *jump, frighten, run, hit*. These are called **active** verbs.

It can tell you a state – what someone **is** – for example, *seem, be, appear, feel*. These are called **stative** verbs.

- **when it is happening**.
  A verb shows if the action or state was in the **past**, or is in the **present**, or will be in the **future**. This is called the **tense** of the verb. For example:
  The security guard **looked** strong. He **terrified** the intruder. (Past tense)
  The security guard **looks** strong. He **is terrifying** the intruder. (Present tense)
  The security guard **will become** strong. He **will terrify** the intruder. (Future tense)

What do adverbs do?

Adverbs tell us more about (**modify**) the verb. They can give us more information about **how**, **when** or **where** something happened.

- **How = adverbs of manner**
  Adverbs of manner give information about how something happened. They are often adjectives with -ly added on the end, such as *slowly, cheerfully, busily, softly*.

- **When = adverbs of time**
  Adverbs of time give information about when something happened. These can be -ly words, such as *immediately, eventually*, but also include words like *today, tomorrow, next*.

- **Where = adverbs of place**
  Adverbs of place give information about where something happened. These are words like *here, there, upstairs, home*.

What do prepositions do?

Prepositions are words which tell us **where** things are:

- The most common use for a preposition is to state **where something is in relation to another object**.

24

Grammar

So, in a sentence, a preposition will always be followed by a noun or pronoun. For example:
*My gloves are **on the table**.*
*The supermarket is **near the DIY warehouse**.*

Common prepositions showing positions of things include: *up, down, in, out, under, over, beside, between, behind, through, against, near, into, with*.

- Prepositions can also tell us **where something is happening**, so they begin some groups of words which have the same function in a sentence as adverbs of place.

- Some prepositions tell us **when something happened**, so they are like adverbs of time. They include words like *since, until, during*.

Sometimes it is hard to tell if a word is being used as an adverb or a preposition. Check if a noun or pronoun follows. If it does, it is a preposition.

For example:
I drifted **down** the stairs. (Preposition)
I drifted **down**. (Adverb)

summary

- Verbs tell us what is happening in a sentence. They may be active or stative. They may be past, present or future in tense.
- Adverbs modify verbs. They can tell us how (manner), when (time) or where (place).
- Prepositions show where one thing is in relation to another.

Questions

1. What is the difference between an active verb and a stative verb?
2. What are the three main verb tenses?
3. Can you spot two adverbs of manner, two adverbs of time and two adverbs of place in this story?

   Taahir walked briskly into the classroom. He was early because he had French. Enthusiastically he took out his homework and immediately showed it to the teacher. Here was where he wanted to be. He was bored elsewhere.

4. What is the most common use for a preposition?

1. Make up three entertaining sentences by choosing one word from each column:
   Make up five more sentences using your own words, but following the same pattern.

2. Choose a topic for a poem of five to ten lines long. Make each line follow the pattern shown on the left:

3. Put different prepositions into these gaps to complete this police statement about Burglar Bill.

   He went ____ the wall and ____ the window ____ the bathroom. Here he tripped ____ the cat. He limped ____ the stairs and ____ the front room. He left ____ the patio doors and stumbled ____ the dustbins. We apprehended him as he struggled ____ the hedge.

   Write your own Burglar Bill story, using as many different prepositions to tell of his activities (and accidents) as you possibly can.

Preposition	Noun
e.g. Beneath	the water

Noun	Verb	Adverb
mermaids	swim	gracefully

Take a piece of your own writing – preferably an adventurous tale or story with lots of action – and redraft it so every verb is modified by at least one adverb of manner. See if you can add excitement by beginning some sentences with prepositions such as 'Across the mountains I travelled ...'.

Pronoun	Verb	Noun	Adverb	Preposition	Noun
I/We/ You/She/ He/They	pulled/ stuffed/ posted	the cat/ a letter/ your hat	carefully/ quickly/ thoughtlessly	into/ up/ through	the letter box a drainpipe the chimney

For more information on verbs and verb tenses see pages 26–27
For more information about adverbs see pages 20–21

Verbs – Tenses and Phrases

intro

Sometimes you will have to look for more than one word to identify the entire verb in a sentence. Read on to discover what goes into making a **verb phrase**, and what we use them for.

> These pages are about verb tenses and verb phrases.

Verb tenses

The three main **verb tenses** are the **past, present and future**. This piece of writing is in the present tense – it sounds as if it is happening right now.

*The security guard **looks** very strong. He **frightens** an intruder. The intruder **is** surprised, but still he **escapes**. As quickly as possible, he **jumps** into his get-away car and **speeds** off down the road. The guard **seems** pleased that he **does** his job well.*

First, can you think how to change the words in bold to make the story sound **as if it happened a long time ago**? (Add words like *had*, *was* or *did* to these **main verbs**.)

Next, see if you can think of alterations to the words in bold so the story sounds **as if it might happen in the future**. (You can use words such as *will*, *might* or *could* as well as the **main verbs**.)

What is a verb phrase?

It is a group of words that does the same job as a verb in a sentence – exactly the sort of groups of words you have just worked out.

- It tells **what is happening** – the action, or the state.
- More important, it tells **when** the events happened.

When we write about **the past** or **the future**, very often we need more than one word to make the verb tense clear. You have found this out already.

What are the names of the parts of a verb phrase?

A **verb phrase** is made up from two different kinds of verb. The **main verb** tells us the action or the state. Other words help show the tense of the verb.

These are called **auxiliary verbs** because they help the main verb. For example, *he will be* (auxiliary) *going* (main) *on holiday*.

Verb participles

Main verbs sometimes change their spelling when you make them into past or present tense verb phrases. These forms of the main verb are called **participles**, because they are only part of the verb. Without the right auxiliary verbs, they are not complete.

Past participles often just add *-ed* to the **main verb stem** (the simplest present tense form of a verb). These are **regular verbs**, because they follow this simple rule, for example, *roast -ed, boil -ed, mash-ed* as in:

I have roasted these potatoes because last time, although I had boiled and mashed them carefully, no one had eaten any at the end of the meal.

At the end of this sentence you will see an **irregular** past participle – *eaten*. Some of the most frequently used verbs have irregular endings which are different for the past tense and the past participle. For example:

Stem	Past tense	Past participle
eat	ate	eaten
ring	rang	rung
give	gave	given
write	wrote	written
go	went	gone

In some British dialects, people use the past tense for every past participle – even for irregular verbs.

Grammar

Do you find it acceptable to say any of these things?

These are dialect expressions. You need to know the standard English past participles – *I have written ...;* *I have given ...; I have eaten... .*

Present participles add *-ing* to the main verb stem. Although they are called 'present', these participles can be used in past, present and future verb phrases to show that something happens for a long time. These are called **continuous** tenses. For example:

I was walking for hours. (**Past continuous** tense)
I am doing my homework. (**Present continuous** tense)
You will be doing this homework for a whole year.
(**Future continuous** tense)

The **infinitive** is the name we give the main verb stem, with no special ending. We write this as *to walk, to fall, to think.*

Auxiliary verbs

These help main verbs to form past and future tenses. They also have the following uses:

- They tell you something is a **possibility** (*I might win the lottery*).
- They can turn sentences round, so the subject of the sentence has the verb done to it. This is called a **passive verb** (*The child was being licked by the dog*).

For more information on verbs, adverbs and prepositions see pages 24–25

summary

- A verb phrase is a group of words which does the job of a verb in a sentence.
- Past and future tense verbs are quite often verb phrases.
- A verb phrase will have: a participle form of the main verb (past participle or present participle) and one or more auxiliary verbs.
- Auxiliary verbs are also used to turn an active verb into a passive verb.

Questions

1 What is the difference between a main verb and a verb phrase?
2 Name the two participle forms and give an example of each one, from these pages.
3 Why do we need auxiliary verbs? Give three different examples from these pages.

1 Underline all the words which make up the verb phrases in these sentences and write down whether they are past, present or future tense:
a) The beautiful princess had been shut in the tower for years.
b) A handsome prince came riding through the woods.
c) 'He is coming to help her escape,' said the jealous fairy.
d) 'I am going to enchant him to make him forget her.'
2 Make these verbs into their irregular past participle form (using standard English).
a) I have [bring] you a glass of beer, Dad.
b) Have you [buy] me that new CD?
c) I have [write] a really good poem for my English homework.
d) So why haven't you [give] me a present yet?

Find a magazine or newpaper. Cut out your own horoscope and a couple of others (choose them for members of your family, or friends). Take three different colour pens or highlighters. Underline or highlight past tense verb phrases in one colour; underline or highlight present tense verb phrases in the second colour; underline or highlight future tense verb phrases in the third colour. Which verb tense is used most often?

27

Simple and Compound Sentences

intro — It is not quick or easy to explain what a **sentence** is. Read on and you will begin to understand why. You will also be learning about **phrases** and **connectives** and the work they do in different kinds of sentence.

> These pages are about the grammar of sentences and explain how phrases are put together in simple sentences.

What can a sentence do?
Sentences can be very different in shape and size, but there are only four types:

- **A statement** – the most common sort of sentence, one which states information. (*The dog chases the children.*)
- **A question** – a sentence which asks for an answer. (*What is happening in the street?*)
- **A command** – a sentence which orders someone (whose name is often not mentioned) to do something. (*Look at us, dad!*)
- **An exclamation** – these sentences are more often spoken than written and express strong feelings. (*Goodness gracious!*)

Simple sentences
The simplest written sentence only has one word. That word will be a verb, and it will be a command. *Run!* It is very unusual indeed to find written sentences without a main verb.

Most simple sentences also tell you the **subject** – a noun naming the person or thing that the sentence is about. For example:

The dog (subject) *runs* (verb).

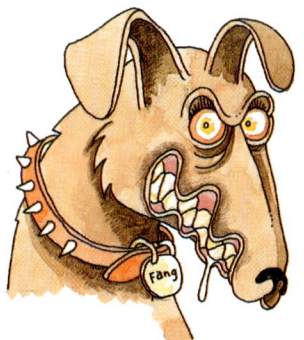

A simple sentence may tell you the **object** – a noun naming someone or something that has the verb done to it. For example:

The dog (subject) *bites* (verb) *Jane* (object).

A simple sentence may also include an **adverb** – which tells you how, where or when the verb was done. For example:

The dog (subject) *bites* (verb) *Jane* (object) *viciously* (adverb).

All simple sentences follow this basic pattern, though you can organise the bits of the sentence in a different order, to add variety to your writing. Can you spot the subject, the verb and the adverb in this sentence? *Afterwards came the surprise.*

What is a phrase?
A **phrase** is a group of words which does the job of a subject, object, verb or adverb in a sentence.

A **noun phrase** does the same job as the subject and object in a sentence. Noun phrases are discussed on page 23.

A **verb phrase** is a group of words that does the job of the verb. Verb phrases are discussed on pages 26–27.

An **adverbial phrase** does the job of an adverb. Adverbs are discussed on pages 24–25.

All of the examples on this page are simple sentences. They follow the same basic pattern. Each sentence has just one main verb.

Grammar

Connectives and compound sentences

If we only wrote in simple sentences, it would sound very jerky, as well as being boring. **Connectives** (sometimes called **conjunctions**) are words we can use to join words, phrases or sentences together. The most common connective is *and*. The most common **compound sentence** is two simple sentences joined by the word *and*. For example:

The dog runs and it bites Jane.

Sometimes you need a more formal word than the everyday *and*. Other words you can use include: *also, additionally, moreover, furthermore.*

Some compound sentences make a **comparison** between two statements using the connective *but*.

For example:

Fred likes the dog but Jane hates it.

More formal words to show contrast are: *however, although, nevertheless.*

Some compound sentences show **time relationships**. For example:

The dog bit Jane then she kicked it.

Time words are especially useful when you are writing a story. There are many time connectives. Here are just a few: *meanwhile, later, simultaneously, before, eventually.*

summary

- A simple sentence must have a main verb. It may also have any, or all, of: a subject, an object, an adverb.
- A phrase is a group of words which does the same job in a sentence as the subject, verb, object or adverb.
- A connective, or conjunction, is a word (and, but, so, then, etc.) used to join other words, phrases or sentences together.
- A compound sentence is made by joining two or more simple sentences together with connectives.

Questions

A

1. What example is given above of the shortest grammatical sentence?
2. What are the other three bits you may find in a simple sentence?
3. Three different kinds of phrase are named on these pages. What are they?
4. What is another name for connectives? What are the most common connectives?

B

1. Decide if the groups of words that follow are sentences or phrases. If they are sentences, copy them out with correct punctuation. If they are phrases, add words of your own to make them into grammatical simple sentences.
   a) the dog buried its bone in the garden
   b) on the motorway a terrible accident
   c) the man in the smart grey suit
   d) quickly she turned off the television
   e) you in the grey sweatshirt turn round now
   f) through the window

2. Choose suitable formal connectives from the lists given on this page to join together the following pairs of simple sentences.
   a) This man is a notorious criminal. He is not sorry for what he has done.
   b) The witness intended to arrive in good time for the trial. The train was delayed for over an hour.
   c) The accused will serve a long sentence in jail. He will be properly punished.
   d) Now you may leave. I never want to see you here again.

C

Write an account of a trip or a holiday that you enjoyed. Try to vary your sentences, so you have a good mixture of short simple sentences and compound sentences which use interesting connectives.

For more information on phrases see pages 22–23 and 26–27

Complex Sentences

intro

A **clause** is a group of words which includes a main verb, but is only a part of a sentence. A complex sentence is any sentence which is made up of two or more clauses.

> These pages explain the difference between a clause and a phrase, and show how two or more clauses may be combined into complex sentences.

The definition of a sentence as 'a group of words that make complete sense' is not always helpful. Some clauses 'make complete sense', but they are not sentences. Read this sentence.

Their first pause was at the Crown Inn, an inconsiderable house, though the principal one of the sort, where a couple of pairs of post-horses were kept, more for the convenience of the neighbourhood than from any run on the road; and his companions had not been expected to be detained by any interest excited there; but in passing it they gave the history of the large room visibly added; it had been built many years ago for a ballroom, and while the neighbourhood had been in a particularly populous, dancing state, had been occasionally used as such; – but such brilliant days had passed away, and now the highest purpose for which it was ever wanted was to accommodate a whist club established amongst the gentlemen and half-gentlemen of the place.

from *Emma* by Jane Austen

Main clauses and subordinate clauses

A **main clause** is a 'complete idea' which could stand on its own. The opening words of this sentence are a main clause:

'Their first pause was at the Crown Inn.'

These words on their own are a grammatical simple sentence. However, in Jane Austen's sentence, these words are the main clause. The rest of her sentence adds more (much more!) information about the Crown Inn.

A **subordinate clause** has a subject and a verb, but it does not make sense on its own, because it refers back to the main clause:

'where a couple of pairs of post-horses were kept'

is just one example of a subordinate clause in Jane Austen's sentence. You need to know the main clause to understand that 'where' refers to the Crown Inn.

One main clause can have more than one subordinate clause linked to it.

Noun clauses, adjectival clauses and adverbial clauses

Subordinate clauses can do the same work in a sentence as **phrases**. The easy way to tell a phrase from a clause is that a clause always has a main verb, and a phrase does not.

You should be able to spot three different types of clause: a **noun clause**, an **adjectival clause** and an **adverbial clause**.

A noun clause may be used as either the subject or the object of the sentence. For example:

Who damaged your calculator is impossible for me to say. (The subject)
The girls said *what they really wanted*. (The object)

Grammar

An adjectival clause will add descriptive detail to a noun. For example:

The boys, *who were all very good-looking*, danced energetically. (Adds detail to the subject)
We enjoyed watching one boy, *whom everyone admired*. (Adds detail to the object – this is why '*whom*' is the link word instead of '*who*')

An adverbial clause does the same work as an adverb – it gives more detail about a verb: how, when or where. It can also tell why. Just like an adverb, this kind of subordinate clause may begin or end a sentence. For example:

The girls sang their song *as loudly as they could*.
(How – **adverbial clause of manner**)
While the girls finished their song, the audience cheered.
(When – **adverbial clause of time**)
People stood *where they had a good view*.
(Where – **adverbial clause of place**)
In order to see better, some people stood on the seats.
(Why – **adverbial clause of reason**)

Complex sentences

Complex sentences are made up of one main clause and one, or more, subordinate clauses. The examples of noun, adjectival and adverbial clauses on this page are complex sentences.

There are some connectives which are only used in complex sentences, where they begin adverbial clauses. **Time connectives** of this kind include: *until, whenever, whilst*. **Logical connectives** include: *because (of), owing to, in order to*.

Jane Austen's sentence is an example of a **coordinated complex sentence**. This means it has more than one main clause, linked by coordinating connectives (for example, '*… but such brilliant days had passed away…*'), as well as quite a number of subordinate clauses.

summary

- A clause is a part of a sentence which includes a main verb.
- A main clause makes complete sense and could stand alone.
- A subordinate clause depends on a main clause to make sense. Subordinate clauses can do the same work as a noun, an adjective or an adverb in a sentence.
- A complex sentence consists of one main clause linked to one or more subordinate clauses.

Questions

A

1. What is the difference between a phrase and a clause?
2. How does a main clause differ from a subordinate clause?
3. What are the different kinds of adverbial clause?
4. What is a complex sentence?
5. How does a complex sentence differ from a complex coordinated sentence?

B

1. Copy out just the main clause from each of these sentences.
a) As soon as Jane bought the book, she started to read it.
b) Jane, who had always liked reading, finished the book before the bus arrived.
c) Jane liked a story which had a happy ending.
d) Jane lent her new book to a boy whom she liked.
e) Because he enjoyed reading, the boy was very grateful.

2. Now write down a list of the subordinate clauses in each of the above five sentences. Write down whether each is doing the job of a noun, an adjective or an adverb in the sentence.

3. Write five complex sentences about members of your family, or your friends. Use the examples given on these pages to make sure you experiment with a variety of different kinds of subordinate clause, and different ordering of clauses in your sentences.

C

Redraft a piece of your own writing, preferably something with quite a bit of description of people and places. Think hard about the effects you can make by varying your sentence structures between short, simple sentences, compound sentences and complex sentences.

For more information on simple and compound sentences see pages 28–29

Commas and Full Stops

> **Commas** and **full stops** are used rather like pauses in speech. They divide strings of words into groups that make sense. Commas mark off groups of words within a sentence. Full stops are used to mark the ends of sentences. That sounds easy, but in real life, sentences can be so different in length and structure that getting full stops and commas in all the right places can be a challenge.

These pages are about basic punctuation of sentences.

Commas

A comma shows you need to have a brief pause within a sentence. Commas are the most common punctuation marks of all, but they are the hardest to learn to use properly because of all the different places they can go.

- When two or more **simple sentences** are joined together, you need a comma before the joining word. Usually, you do not put a comma before the word *and*. Joining words to look out for include: *but, so, then, because*. For example:

    They thought they would have a good holiday, but they were wrong.

- When a sentence has a **phrase** inserted into the middle of it, commas are used rather like brackets. Check this by removing the words inside the commas – the rest of the sentence will still make sense. For example:

    The weather, to our delight, was warm and sunny. (Note: if you put in the first comma, it is wrong to miss out the second – like having just the first bracket.)

- When sentences have more than one **clause** in them, there is a comma to separate the clauses. For example:

    If you carry on like that, you will be in serious trouble.

Lists

Commas separate words in lists of nouns, adjectives or verbs. For example:

We bought a cream cake, some ice cream, chocolate and jelly. (Nouns)

Mr George put on a large, curly, white beard and pretended to be Santa Claus. (Adjectives)

The children looked, cheered, ran and grabbed the goodies. (Verbs)

Direct speech

A comma may be needed before you open speech marks. For example:

Samina asked me, 'How long will you be?'

A comma may even come at the end of a sentence, if it is used just before you close speech marks. For example:

'I'm almost ready to go,' I replied.

Capital letters and full stops

This is probably the millionth time you have been reminded that **all sentences must start with a capital letter and finish with a full stop**. Just about as many times, you will have been told that **a sentence is a group of words that makes complete sense**.

Here are some sentences, just to show you how different they can be and to demonstrate why getting full stops right is not straightforward:

Run.
Jo ran.
Sian saw Jo.
The boy from the next street also saw Jo running.
A few minutes later, the boy went across the road to where Sian was still standing.

Question marks and **exclamation marks** have built in full stops. They are used to show the ends of particular kinds of sentence.

Punctuation of Sentences

You might find you need to use these in any kind of writing, but they are most needed when you are writing out **direct speech**, or a script. There is no need to use a full stop as well as a question mark or exclamation mark. But you do need to remember both are followed by a capital letter, just like a full stop.

Other uses for full stops

- **Three in a row (...)** shows something is missed out. This might be because someone is cut off before they finish speaking:

  Help me! I can't swi...

Or you might want to have a mystery ending on a story:

That was the last time Jim was ever seen, though there are tales in the village about the lake being haunted,...

Or you might want to miss some words out to make a quotation shorter. For example:

Romeo compares Juliet to 'torches ... a rich jewel ... a snowy dove ...'

- **Full stops to shorten words** – some words can be cut short. For example:

  Professor – Prof.   Lancashire – Lancs.
  Monday – Mon.   November – Nov.

Names of people and organisations can be cut down to the first letters. For example:

David Herbert Lawrence – D. H. Lawrence
Youth Hostel Association – Y.H.A.

These are called **abbreviations**.
A full stop shows the word has been shortened.

summary

Commas have two main uses:
- to separate phrases and clauses within a sentence
- to separate single words, or phrases, in a list.

Full stops have two main uses:
- to mark the end of every sentence
- to show that words, or letters, have been cut out.

Questions

A

1. Make a list – as long as you like, providing it has commas in the right places – starting:
   For my birthday I received ...
2. Apart from lists, where else would you need to use commas?
3. Explain three different uses for full stops.
4. Write abbreviations for these words, correctly punctuated: Reverend, Street, Leicestershire, People's Dispensary for Sick Animals, United States of America.
5. Which other punctuation marks are followed by a capital letter and why?

B

1. Where do these sentences need commas?
   a) When we get to school let's go on the field.
   b) We could do that or we could look for Pat.
   c) Pat unlike me hates football.
   d) If we can find Sam we could all have a great time.
2. Which of these groups of words is a proper sentence, needing a capital letter and full stop? Write them out, correctly punctuated. Then complete the unfinished sentences and punctuate those.
   a) sailing on the lake
   b) they stopped
   c) the boat was leaking
   d) now they need to

C

Rewrite the story below, deciding which of the commas need to be full stops. Add any missing commas, question marks or exclamation marks.

It was a cold dark rainy night, Aimee and Kris were late home, so they decided to take a short cut through the graveyard, they had not gone far when a sudden noise made them jump, a strange high-pitched hooting screeching sound, 'Whatever was that' Aimee whispered, Kris, with horror all over his face looked at her, 'No, it's not possible' he screamed

Continue this story using your own ideas. Make use of everything you have revised about how to punctuate sentences accurately.

For more information on sentence structure see pages 28–31
For more information on direct speech see pages 36–37

Apostrophes, Colons and Semi-colons

*As your writing becomes more mature, you will find you need to extend the range of punctuation you use. The **apostrophe** is explained here. Read carefully, as many people get very confused about these. Also, you will be introduced to **colons** and **semi-colons**, the punctuation marks you need to use once you begin to put together complex sentences.*

These pages are about more advanced punctuation skills.

What are apostrophes?

Apostrophes look rather like commas, but appear at the top of a word, rather than on the line. They are often used in the wrong places.

There are only two purposes for apostrophes:

- In informal speech or writing, words can be shortened. Apostrophes are used to show where a letter is missed, to represent the shorter way of saying a word.
- Apostrophes are also used to show that someone (or something) is the owner of an object.

The writer George Bernard Shaw wanted to ban 'missing letter' apostrophes and refused to use them himself. Look at his plays and you will see this is true.

Missing letters

These are also called **contractions** or **omissions**. The most common one of all is *not*, which becomes *n't*. The apostrophe replaces the letter 'o'. The *n't* joins the word which comes before *not*. The two words are written as one, but their spelling does not change.

are not	aren't	could not	couldn't
did not	didn't	had not	hadn't
does not	doesn't	is not	isn't

One common mistake is to write things like '*dosent*' or '*hadent*'. Another is putting the apostrophe in between the words like '*did'nt*' or '*are'nt*'. Avoid this!

More unusual contractions include:

I am	I'm	it is	it's
we are	we're	you will	you'll
let us	let's	will not	won't

Ownership

This is also called **possession**. You put an apostrophe after the owner's name, and before the final 's', to show ownership. For example:

*The **dog's dinner** is ready.*
***Jane's coat** has gone missing.*
***Britain's climate** is awful.*
*A **knife's blade** is sharp.*

If the owner's name already ends with an 's', or if it is a plural word that ends with an 's', the apostrophe comes after the 's'. For example:

***James' coat** has gone missing.*
***All knives' blades** are sharp.*
***Charles Dickens' novels** are mostly very long.*
***Babies' nappies** smell awful.*

34

Punctuation of Sentences

What are colons and semi-colons?

Colons and semi-colons mark pauses in longer, more complex sentences where a comma would not quite be enough. You can manage without colons and semi-colons, but there are places where they can make your writing more effective, once you know what they are for.

Colons are used to introduce extra information in a sentence. You will find them in three places:

- To introduce lists. For example:
  Your walker's first-aid kit needs to include: plasters, antiseptic ointment, insect repellent and elastic bandages.
- To show where the second half of a sentence expands or explains the first half. For example:
  It was a cold night: torrential rain was falling and there was a bitter wind.
- To show that the words that follow are a quotation. For example:
  As the old saying goes: too many cooks spoil the broth.

Semi-colons break up sentences consisting of two or more **clauses**. They may be used:

- instead of a full stop to link two or more sentences. For example: *The wind howled; an owl hooted; a dark, shapeless figure crossed the lawn.*
- between two clauses, especially when words such as nevertheless, moreover, otherwise begin the second clause. For example: *He leaned against the old, oak door with all his weight; nevertheless it remained firmly closed.*
- to separate items in a list when the items are longer than a single word. For example: *Many noises scare me after dark: the sound of footsteps behind me, when I'm walking alone; creaking floorboards, sounding as if someone is walking around my house; the wailing of fighting cats, and the hooting of owls.*

summary

- **Apostrophes mark: a letter missed out of a contracted word; the owner of something.**
- **Colons introduce extra information in complex sentences.**
- **Semi-colons separate closely linked clauses in complex sentences.**
- **Colons and semi-colons do not need to be followed by a capital letter – they mark a break in a sentence, not the end of a sentence.**

Questions

A

In sentences a–c, replace the missing apostrophes. In sentences d and e, decide where to use colons and semi-colons.

a) Im very surprised that you havent got ready – its late enough now.
b) At eleven oclock we will visit Hadrians wall, provided were on time.
c) Is this Johns coat, or is it James or one of the other boys?
d) Your packed lunch includes some egg and mayonnaise sandwiches a packet of prawn cocktail flavour crisps some chocolate digestive biscuits and several types of fresh fruit.
e) Preparations are complete the coach is waiting the children are about to begin their trip.

B

1 Some people get the wrong idea about apostrophes and start to put them before every single 's', and in between every 'n' and 't', even when no letter is missed out. Sometimes these are called 'greengrocer's apostrophes', because you see them on handwritten signs in shops. Rewrite this school dinner menu with no unnecessary apostrophes.

2 Write an opening paragraph for a thrilling story (mystery, horror or ghost story). Punctuate at least one of your sentences with semi-colons to create tension and at least one sentence with a colon to introduce extra information, or a quotation.

TUESDAY'S CHOICE'S.

Fruit juice's - orange
Sandwiche's - cheese and pickle's or Chef''s Special
Ploughman's lunch.
Pizza's - cheese and mushroom's
Shepherd's pie
Lamb with min't sauce
Baked bean's
Tomatoe's
Chip's
Yoghurt - s'berry or r'berry
Eve's pudding and custard

C

Find some examples of apostrophes, semi-colons and colons being used – correctly, or wrongly – in newspapers, signs, books or magazines you read. Write down, and comment on, things you notice.

For more information on complex sentences see pages 30–31

Inverted commas

intro

When we write out the exact words spoken in a conversation, it is called **direct speech**. To punctuate speech correctly, you need to know how to use **inverted commas**, and other punctuation marks.

> These pages are about how to set out and punctuate direct speech correctly.

Inverted commas are often called **speech marks**.
They mark the words someone spoke. They have exactly the same function as speech bubbles in cartoons or photo-stories. First, read this cartoon.

Next, read how the same conversation might look written as direct speech.

(2a) 'Welcome back to the racing at Sandown Park,' (4c) came the voice from the television.

(1) 'Dad, look! I've found a book that shows you how to hypnotise people and make them obey you!' shouted Jenny, excitedly. 'What do you think? Can I try it on you?' (2b)

There was no reply. 'Mum, Dad's watching the races again! Shall I hypnotise him and make him do the washing up?' continued Jenny, as mother came in.

(1) As she rolled up the racing pages, mother exclaimed, (3) 'Thank you, Jenny, Mum can deal with this!' (5)

(4b) 'Hey!! What was that?' shrieked father, as she hit him on the back of the head. (4a)

Now read the rules for how to set out speech, and look to see how the rules have been followed in the story.

Basic rules for perfect punctuation of speech

1. Start a new line for each new speaker. Indent it from the margin (like a new paragraph).
2. a Open inverted commas before the first spoken word. These can look like " or '.
   b Close inverted commas after the last spoken word. These match the opening ones " or '.
3. The first word after you open inverted commas usually starts with a capital letter.
4. There is always a punctuation mark **before** you close inverted commas. This punctuation mark can be:
   a a question mark (?) if the spoken words were a question
   b an exclamation mark (!) if the spoken words were emphasised, for example, loud, or an order, or an expression of emotion.
   c a comma (,) when the speaker is named straight after the spoken words
   d a full stop (.) when the speaker is not named. Instead the spoken words are followed by either the words of another speaker or a completely new sentence.
5. When the speaker is named before you write the spoken words, put a comma (,) immediately before you open the inverted commas.

36

Other uses for inverted commas

Titles. Inverted commas are used to mark the titles of all kinds of things: books, films, newspapers, television programmes, etc. For example:

I usually read 'The Daily Telegraph' and I always watch 'The News at Ten'.

It is important to remember that titles also need capital letters on the main words.

> **H**
>
> It is especially important to remember the inverted commas when the title is also the name of a person in a book or film, so we can tell if you mean the person or the story. For example, I saw 'Dracula' at the weekend. This probably means the film!

Thoughts. Sometimes writers may use inverted commas in the same way as speech marks to mark the exact words someone is thinking. Thoughts may also need to be punctuated with question marks and exclamation marks.

Quotation marks. If a speaker repeats the exact words someone else said, or wrote, put these inside inverted commas. Usually, in printed books, double inverted commas ("...") are used to show quotations like these. Single inverted commas are used in direct speech ('...') When you quote exact words from something you have read, for example as evidence in a comprehension answer, or in a literature essay, inverted commas are used as quotation marks.

summary

Inverted commas are used to show you are writing down someone else's words. They have four main uses:
- to mark words spoken in direct speech
- to mark someone's thoughts
- to show you are quoting someone's written or spoken words
- to mark titles of books, films, television programmes, etc.

Questions

A

1. What are the main uses for inverted commas? What do they have in common?
2. Cover the numbers round the story and see if you can work out which rule each of the arrows is pointing out.
3. Which four punctuation marks might you need to use **before** you close inverted commas?
4. What is the difference between seeing Hercules and seeing 'Hercules'?
5. What two other names are often given to inverted commas? Why?

B

1. Write a conversation, beginning with this part of the cartoon. Make sure you obey all the rules 1–5.

   I shall hypnotise these kids and make them obey me!

2. Write a conversation of your own invention, following the rules for layout and punctuation of speech. Ideas might include: an argument with your brother/sister or a discussion with your teacher about why you haven't done your homework.

C

It is often a good idea to avoid repeating 'said' when you write a long piece of direct speeech. First check alternatives used on page 36. Then look up the words *say*, *speak* and *talk* in your thesaurus to find other verbs you can use instead. You will find useful adverbs as you do so.

Paragraphs

intro

Paragraphs group together sentences which are closely connected in meaning. In a long piece of writing, paragraphs break up complicated sequences of events or ideas into organised, manageable chunks to make it easier for readers to understand. When you write at length, you need to group your sentences into paragraphs so that someone reading your work will not miss the point.

> These pages are about what paragraphs are and why we need to organise longer pieces of writing in paragraphs.

What do paragraphs look like?

If you are handwriting, when you decide it is right to end your old paragraph and start a new one, you put a full stop, go down to the next line on your paper, and indent (this means you start to write about 1–2 cm to the right of the margin). So paragraphed handwriting looks like this:

> *90% of our waste ends up on rubbish tips where it pollutes the earth, the rivers and the air, and our wildlife.*
>
>   *Do your bit to help – find out where your local recycling centre is. Put glass in your bottle bank. Recycle your paper and aluminium cans.*
>
>   *Remember, rubbish left behind can pollute rivers and hurt animals. Gates left open can hurt livestock. Walking across fields can damage crops.*

Topic sentences

Every paragraph has one important sentence which is central to what it is about. This is called the **topic sentence**. The other sentences add more details about the topic sentence. Any sentence that is not about the topic sentence is in the wrong paragraph. Often the topic sentence is at the beginning of a paragraph, like this:

Tartar will form on your cat's teeth if you feed it too much sweet or sloppy food. This can cause no end of trouble. If you notice your cat is eating very slowly or dribbling from the mouth, examine the teeth carefully. Usually there will be symptoms of foul breath, inflamed and swollen gums and often an abcess.

from ***The Pan Book of Cats*** by Rose Tenant

In this paragraph, the topic sentence is not at the beginning. Can you see which sentence it is?

Back to the question of food, appetites vary, so it is difficult to say just how much your cat will need. One thing is certain: a healthy cat has a good appetite. Your cat may need more food than the average person realises. One hundred to one hundred and fifty grams of fresh meat daily, divided into two equal portions, with added brown bread scraps, or cereal, or vegetables, if your cat will eat them. Never give cats potato or white bread.

Paragraphs in stories

In **narrative writing** – the kind of writing which tells a story, where events happen over a period of time – like a **short story**, or a piece of **autobiographical writing**, the most likely reason for grouping sentences in a paragraph is that they give you more details about the same event. When something new starts to happen, you need to start a new paragraph.

Sometimes paragraphs mark a change of focus. You may have been writing about what is happening in a particular place, and then the action moves to a new place. Or time may pass, and connective phrases like '*a few minutes later*' or '*the next morning*' may be the signal for a new paragraph.

Here is an autobiographical piece, written by Shamim. She has just begun Year 9. When she gets carried away by her ideas, she forgets all about paragraphs, as she has here, writing about her cousin's wedding in Pakistan. As you read, decide where a new event, or a new time, deserved to be marked by a paragraph.

Punctuation of Sentences

I was about four when I went to my uncle's son's wedding. I thought it was very stupid having weddings at night. During the day we were busy sewing our dresses and we decorated our hands with henna, so at night we were ready to go to the wedding. We went up the hill and down to the other side until we came to the village called Uppla-Murch. The bridegroom hadn't arrived yet, the bride was in a room where no man could see her. My mum and I went in and saw her. She was loaded with gold, earrings, necklaces, bangles, rings and tickha (star shapes). The bride wore a bright red coloured dress, and a long big red scarf which her face was covered in. She could not see anything at all. We went out and the bridegroom arrived. The priest was already there. The bride came out with her friends and she sat next to the groom. The hacka (which means that if she would have him as her husband and he has her as his wife) was done by the priest. When they finished the priest took the bride's scarf and fastened it on to the groom's scarf and after this they were both walking around together. After the ceremony we had our feast: we had pakora, chapatis, salted rice and sweet rice, curry and so on. After the feast they had more singing and dancing going on. There were rockets and those plastic aeroplanes which you lit from the back zooming off. It was a special day.

from *Extending Literacy* by Wray and Lewis

Paragraphs in factual writing

Writing which explains facts or opinions can be more difficult to paragraph, because you haven't got such clear changes of time and event to help you. The other thing which is a problem with this kind of writing is making sure the paragraphs link together smoothly so the whole piece of writing flows, never sounding jerky or disjointed. **Connectives** — such as *however, also, furthermore* — are very useful here.

summary

A paragraph is a group of sentences which all add details about a topic sentence. The topic sentence of a paragraph tells the reader the main point of that paragraph. In a story, reasons for ending one paragraph and beginning the next might be:
- new event
- new place
- new time
- new person.

In a piece of factual writing, reasons for ending one paragraph and beginning the next might be:
- new idea
- new argument
- new opinion
- a summary or a conclusion of the writing.

Questions

A

1. Why do we need paragraphs?
2. How do you show a new paragraph in handwriting?
3. What are the topic sentences of the two paragraphs about caring for cats?
4. When might you need to start a new paragraph in a story?
5. When might you need to start a new paragraph in a piece of factual writing?

B

1. Look again at Shamim's account of her cousin's wedding. Decide which sentences you think should be the beginning of new paragraphs. (It may help to know that she decided there ought to be six paragraphs in this piece.) Draw a series of pictures, one each for the main idea of every paragraph. Write the opening sentence for the paragraph under each of your pictures.
2. Write your own acount of a special occasion you remember. Shamim's cousin's wedding should give you some ideas for writing. Make sure you organise your account into six to eight paragraphs.

C

Choose an issue that you know arouses strong feelings for and against. Collect some reasons for opinions on both sides of the argument from your family or friends. Write up the discussion in paragraphs.

For more information on connectives see pages 28–29

Reasons for Writing

intro

All writing has a purpose, and some possible purposes are shown in the pictures below. Can you find examples of them in your home – in magazines, leaflets, manuals, letters and books? A piece of writing can have more than one purpose. For example, an anti-drugs leaflet might be designed to inform and persuade. When you write, think of your purpose. If possible, try your writing out on friends and family, not just your teacher.

These pages will show you how to write in a style that fits your reasons for writing and that is suited to your readers.

Sell

Instruct

Inform

Style and purpose

You will need to adjust your style to fit your purpose. The examples below will help you to do this:

'These animals live in the Amazon rainforest. They feed on tree frogs and moths, catching their prey with their long sticky tongues.'
To inform: a straightforward factual statement.

'First insert the long end of the lever under the tyre rim, hooking the notched end round a spoke.'
To instruct: clear, step-by-step account which refers to key parts and methods.

Authoring Skills

'Cigarette advertising should be banned because it encourages young people to become addicted to tobacco at an age when they are likely to ignore the health risks.'

To persuade: the words *should* and *because* are used to show opinion and reason.

'Tired of doing homework every night? The Samsara Homeboy will do it all for you! Just programme Homeboy with subject, task and a sample of your handwriting.'

To sell: uses questions and promises, making it sound simple.

'The inside of our car is a sort of family album on wheels, taking us down memory lane. A sea of Gran's sweet wrappers rustles restlessly underfoot. A dark stain on the rear seat shows where my sister was sick after eating too many Easter eggs last year.'

To entertain: includes images (the family album, the 'sea' of wrappers), sound effects ('wrappers rustles restlessly') and visual details.

Target audience

The second thing to decide is who you're writing for — your **target audience**. For example, are you writing for:

- a particular age group — for young children keep sentences short and the range of words you use (**vocabulary**) simple
- a particular social group, such as girls or boys, parents, or tourists
- people who have specialist knowledge and understand technical terms?

summary

- Your writing style should be suited to your purpose, for example to inform. It should be appropriate for your target audience.

Questions

A

1. What do you think is the most important rule when writing to inform?
2. What is this book's target audience?
3. Name three reasons for writing.
4. Name two ways in which you would adjust your style for young children.

B

1. Identify the purpose of the following:

   'Keep plastic bags away from young children.'

   'Spoon the mixture into a casserole dish and bake for 30 minutes.'

   'Beverly looked up and down the darkened street. A single car crawled past.'

2. Identify the target audience for the following:

   'Billy was a very small, one-eyed bear. He lived at the bottom of the toy box.'

   'So now it's time for my hit-list of gorgeous guys!'

   'City have been facing relegation all season, and tonight they're playing away.'

3. Think of possible dangers in the home. Write a set of safety hints for 8-year-olds.
4. Write an entertaining piece for your own age group on 'How to be popular'.

C

Describe your local area:

a) as if you were an estate agent trying to persuade people to move there (for example, 'This area has a wonderful view of the city...')

b) as if you were appealing for a local grant (for example, 'This area is a hide-out for drug users and our children have nowhere to play...')

c) to entertain (for example, 'Our area has one thing in common with Stonehenge — no one really knows what it's for').

For more information about writing for a target audience see pages 90–91

Planning your Writing

intro

It is important to plan essays and stories. Otherwise you may become confused, miss things out, or get stuck. Even in an exam you should allow 5–10 minutes for this. One method is shown below. Use plain paper, turned sideways if you like. Include images to get your imagination working, and perhaps colour-coding for different kinds of idea. When you have your ideas, number the ones that you decide to use, in the order in which you intend to use them.

These pages are about planning your writing, how to write good beginnings and endings, and drafting.

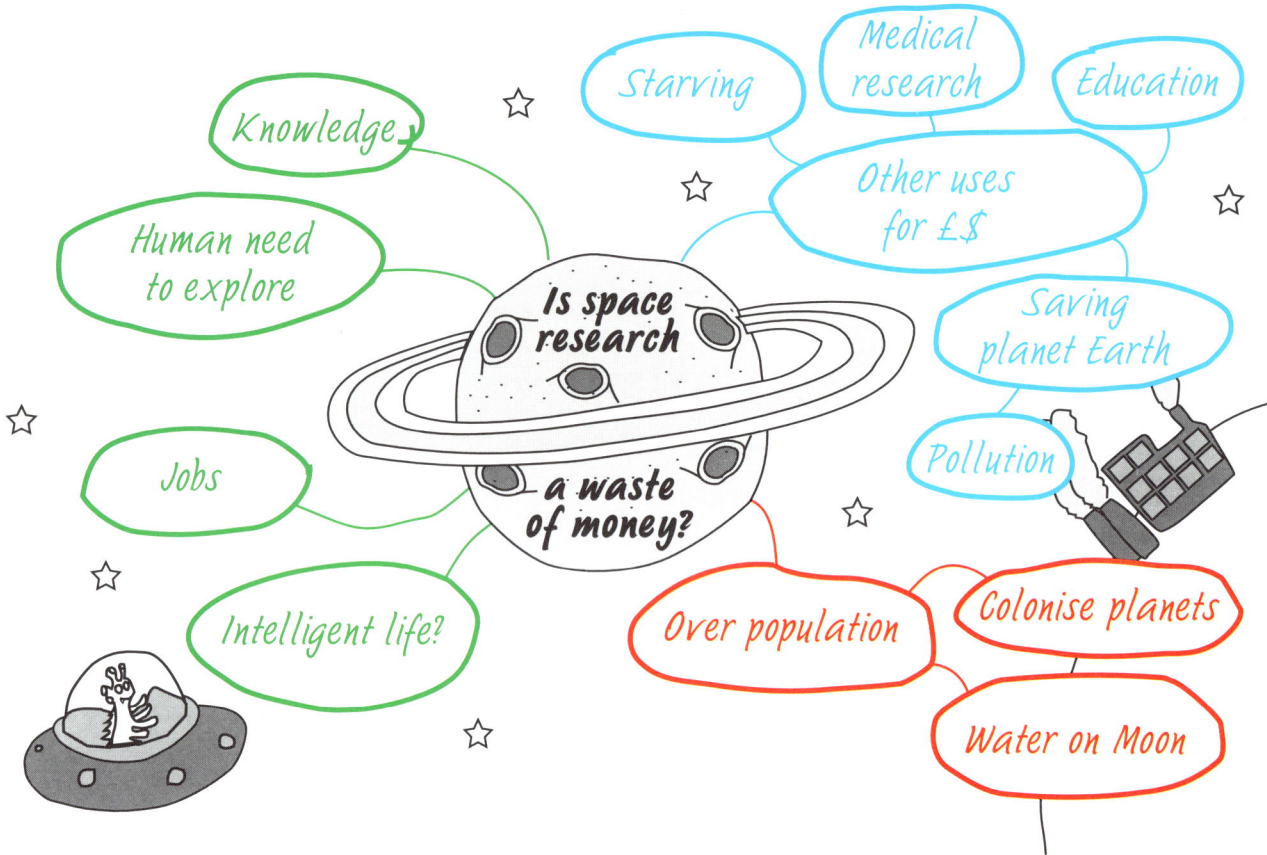

[Mind map centred on "Is space research a waste of money?" with branches:
- *Knowledge*
- *Human need to explore*
- *Jobs*
- *Intelligent life?*
- *Starving*
- *Medical research*
- *Education*
- *Other uses for £ $*
- *Saving planet Earth*
- *Pollution*
- *Over population*
- *Colonise planets*
- *Water on Moon]*

Beginnings

A beginning should catch your reader's interest. With a story, you particularly need to excite curiosity. From the first sentence your reader should be asking questions and wanting to know what happens next. In an essay, you must give a clearer idea of what to expect, but you can still surprise your reader.

Here are some beginnings for our space essay. Decide which you prefer, and why:

'As I look out of my window at the starry night-sky...'

'The US plans to spend a billion dollars exploring Mars over the next three years. During this time, two million children in the world will starve to death.'

'We've come a long way since 12 April 1961, when the Russian astronaut Yuri Gagarin became the first man in space.'

Authoring Skills

Endings

You wouldn't leap across a river without looking to see where you might land, would you? In the same way, you need to have a good idea of how you will end an essay or story before you begin.

Read some story endings. One possibility is the 'unexpected twist', but avoid the over-used 'Then I woke up. It had all been a dream'. Another idea is to leave the reader with a visual image:

'The bird sped from her hands into the blue sky. For a while she strained to track it with her eyes, until the effort grew too much, and it became just one of the distant shapes darting high above the city.'

At the end of an essay, your reader must feel that you have reached a conclusion – not just run out of time or ideas. You may need to give a brief summary in order to do this, but don't just repeat yourself. One technique is to tie the end in with the beginning:

'Outside my window the moon is rising. Perhaps one day, thanks to space research, people will go there on holiday.'

Drafting

Except in an exam, you should write a **first draft** – a first version which you can then improve. If using a computer, print out your first draft and write your changes on to it. See how improvements have been made below:

> Another argument in favour of space research is that before
> ~~Before~~ long our only hope of ~~lasting~~ survival as a
> species may be in space. ~~The numbers of~~
> ~~people of the world,~~ despite war, famine
> and disease, world population continue**s** to soar.
> Unfortunately remains the present
> Earth ~~continues~~ the same old size. At ~~this~~ rate
> it ~~its population~~ will double by the year 2030, ~~roughly.~~

summary
- Planning is essential for most writing.
- Beginnings must gain attention.
- Endings must give a sense of conclusion.
- Mark any major changes that seem necessary on your first draft.

Questions

A
1. Why should you plan an essay?
2. What does the beginning of a story need to do to your reader?
3. Explain what is meant by 'an unexpected twist' in a story.
4. Describe one effective way to end an essay.
5. Name two types of change you might make when rewriting your first draft.

B
1. Plan essays on two of the following: 'Is sport just a pastime?'; 'My room and what it says about me'; 'Vegetarianism – right or wrong?'.
2. Write two possible beginnings and endings for one of the essay titles above.
3. Identify what is attention-catching in each of the space essay beginnings above.
4. Redraft the following. It continues from the drafting example given above. You may need to cross out repetitions, rearrange ideas, find better words, and add description.

'More pollution means more global warming and destruction of the ozone layer that protects the Sun's harmful rays. Increased people means pollution, especially as poor places gets industries in a race to catch up with us and pay off debts.'

C
Plan, draft and redraft an essay or story based on the question, 'What will life in Britain be like in 100 years' time?'

43

Proofreading and Presentation

No book becomes a bestseller just because its spelling, punctuation and grammar are really good or because it doesn't have inky smudges on it. However, if your work is messy and full of mistakes, it makes a bad first impression.

These pages tell you how to check your work for mistakes in spelling, punctuation and grammar, and how to improve your presentation.

Proofreading

Proofreading means checking for mistakes in spelling, punctuation and grammar. It is worth allowing five minutes for this at the end of an exam. For other work allow longer. If you find a lot of small mistakes that make your work messy, or if you decide that bigger changes are needed, consider writing a final corrected draft.

You should check for the following:

- Capitals not used for 'I', names or to start new sentences (see page 32).
- Use of a comma when you should have started a new sentence (see page 32).
- Apostrophes misused (as in 'did'nt' or 'I like dog's' – see page 34).
- Word confusions, especially their/there/they're, whose/who's (see pages 12–13).
- Misspellings, such as the incorrect use of double and single letters (see pages 12–15).
- Awkward word order (try reading aloud).
- Use of dialect expressions when you should have written in standard English (see page 2).

Presentation

Good presentation makes your work easier to read. Use a proper heading and date, underlined with a ruler. Leave a left-hand margin. If your handwriting is very large or messy, use wide-lined paper. Don't split words at line-ends unless you need to save space. Sometimes you might use subheadings and illustrations to make a long piece of work more enjoyable for the reader, especially in a project.

SPACE RESEARCH   19th March

Another argument in favour of space research is that before long our only hope of survival as a species may be in space. Despite war, famine and disease, world population continues to soar. At the present rate it will double by the year 2030. Unfortunately, Earth remains the same old size.

Increased population means more pollution, especially as Third World countries build up industries in a race to catch up with the West and pay off debts. More pollution means more global warming and destruction of the ozone layer that protects us from the Sun's harmful rays.

Could we live on other planets? Water has recently been found on the dark side of the Moon – in a frozen lake. Mars is another possibility, though we might need to build a giant protective dome.

Authoring Skills

Handwriting

Experiment with pens until you find one that suits you. A fountain pen might be best if you can avoid smudging or spilling ink. Failing that, a good-quality felt-tip pen might be neater than a ballpoint.

If possible write at a desk or table, not on your lap or on the floor. If you make a mistake in a final draft, cross it out neatly or use an ink rubber. Cross out the whole word if you have to change more than one letter.

> **Before printing was widespread, no one bothered much about spelling. Shakespeare even spelled his own name in several different ways!**

Word-processing

If you use a computer, you won't have to worry about your handwriting, but you will still need to check spelling, punctuation and grammar. Use your computer's spellcheck to help you, but remember that it will not spot word confusions, such as the use of 'wear' when you meant 'where', and it will not be able to check the spelling of names. You should also make sure that your spellcheck is set to English UK spelling. Do not rely on word-processor grammar checkers, as they are often unhelpful.

You can improve presentation by setting headings in bold or italic typefaces and by inserting a line space before them.

summary
- Proofreading means checking for spelling, punctuation and grammar.
- Good presentation makes your work easier to read.
- Use a good-quality pen and write at a desk or table.
- Computer spellchecks do not catch word confusions.

Questions

A
1. At what stage of writing a piece of work should you proofread it?
2. Name three things that improve presentation.
3. Give three examples of spelling mistakes that computer spellchecks will miss.

B
1. The computer's grammar checker and spellcheck found no problems in the following sentence: 'Karen come threw the door and gave her farther his diner, your grate he said.' Rewrite the sentence using correct punctuation, spelling and grammar.
2. Copy and proofread the following:
Could we live on other plannets. Water has resently been found on the dark side off the Moon in a frozen lake, Mar's is another posibbility though we might need to build a giant protective dame.
3. Write out the main types of proofreading mistake down the left-hand side of a sheet of paper. Look carefully at ten pages or more of your **marked** written work. Each time one type of mistake appears, make a mark next to it on your sheet. Add up the totals to see what kinds of mistake you need to concentrate on.

C
Read the rhyme below and try to predict which mistakes a computer spellcheck would catch. Then type it into a computer and spellcheck it. Were you right? Write out a correct version. Finally, make up a similar rhyme of your own and spellcheck it.

Spell cheques really help you,
Of that yew can be shore.
Accept of coarse they miss sum things,
Witch is an awful boar.

Sew trust a dictionary
If yew want too get it write,
Butt better, learn you're spellings,
Ore yew mite bee up awl knight!

45

Be a Better Listener

intro

Most children learn to talk by listening. Babies listen to the language of their parents and to the many sounds around them and begin to copy them. This is where language starts. As we grow older we continue to learn about the world by listening to the opinions and ideas of others. We can then form ideas of our own and learn to express them clearly.

These pages are about improving your listening skills which will help you in all areas of your English.

Why is listening important?

To be good at English, or any other language for that matter, we need to practise listening carefully and with understanding. If you have ever tried to speak French to a French person, for example, you will know that you may be able to ask a question but listening to the reply and understanding it is much, much harder.

Listening is important therefore because it helps us to:

- be a better speaker
- form opinions
- follow instructions
- learn more quickly
- write more clearly.

Active listening

There is a big difference between hearing and listening. Have you ever been in a situation in class where you have heard what the teacher has said but you have not really been listening? You may have heard the phrase 'The words go in one ear and straight out the other'! This happens when we are not concentrating on what is being said – our minds are somewhere else.

So to be an effective listener we must practise taking an active part, using our brains as well as our ears to understand and respond to what has been said.

Listening practice

Try this simple test. Listen to the news headlines on the radio or television. Then write down the ones that you can remember. You will probably only remember the stories that interest you. Now listen to the news with a notebook so you can note down a few words about each headline – you are now more actively involved in listening and will be able to remember much more.

Note-taking is a very simple but effective way to improve your listening – it helps your brain to concentrate on what is being said.

If you are taking part in a group discussion, you will need to listen very carefully to all the different opinions expressed. To help the discussion along, listening is just as important as speaking.

Speaking and Listening

Another way to listen actively is to ask questions in order to find out more information. It is also very important in this situation to look interested – this will encourage people to talk more and show them that you are really listening.

Look at the following situations.

What might happen if you are **not** actively listening in each case?

- A friend gives you directions to her house and a specific time at which to arrive.
- Your teacher gives you details about an important test that is coming up.
- A technician explains to you the safety rules in a science laboratory.

summary

- Listening is not the same as hearing.
- In conversation and discussions listening is just as important as speaking.
- To listen effectively takes practice.

Questions

A

1. What is the difference between listening and hearing?
2. Why is active listening so important?
3. What are two things you can do to become a better active listener?

B

1. How does listening help us to be better speakers of English?
2. Give three reasons why we might not listen as carefully as we should.
3. Describe in detail a situation where not listening might get someone into trouble.
4. Listen to a programme on the radio or watch a programme on television where you need to listen to what is said, for example, a drama, news, documentary, science, wildlife programme, etc. Write a review of the programme describing what you found out and what was said.

C

1. Make a poster which is designed to encourage people to be better listeners. Make it bright and colourful using both pictures and written advice.
2. Prepare an advice sheet for pupils about improving their listening skills. This sheet should help students who are going to have a speaking and listening test.

Interviewing

These pages are about how to conduct an effective interview.

intro

Interviewing can take many different forms – from an informal question and answer session with a friend to a very formal situation with a famous person. Being able to conduct an interview with confidence will help you to find out a great variety of information and will improve your speaking and listening skills.

Preparing the questions

When preparing your questions it is very important to be clear about what it is you want to find out from the person you are interviewing. It is also just as important that your questions are clear and easy to understand. If you get the wrong information or if your questions cannot be understood, then the interview will not go well.

Closed questions and open questions

A **closed question** only allows a very limited response. For example:

- What is your favourite colour?
- When is your birthday?
- Do you have any brothers and sisters?

This type of question can usually be answered in one or two words and is useful for finding out facts. They can be used at the beginning of an interview to get some basic information and to help 'break the ice'.

An **open question** asks for opinions or ideas or feelings, so you will get a much wider variety of answers. For example:

- What do you think about fox-hunting?
- Why do you think more young girls are taking up smoking?
- How did you get interested in football/dance/music/conservation?

This type of question may need to be carefully aimed at the interests of the person you are interviewing. There is no point asking someone to talk to you about football if he or she knows nothing about it.

Conducting the interview

Interviewing somebody can be quite a nerve-racking experience for both the interviewer and the interviewee! Therefore it is a good idea to be well prepared and to try to create a positive and relaxing atmosphere.

A checklist of things to consider might include the following:

- What will be the best seating arrangements?
- Is it possible to provide drinks?
- What is the best way to encourage talking? Through eye contact, smiling, helping the person out with difficult questions.
- Being ready to change the questions if they are not going well or if more explanation is needed.
- Listening to the answers with interest and responding to them by nodding or making a point of your own.
- Being prepared for all sorts of different responses – some people will not stop talking, others will hardly say a word.
- It is your responsibility to make the interview work, not the interviewee's.

H

For an interview to go well it is up to the person asking the questions to make the guest feel relaxed and to encourage them to provide the information that the interviewer wants. Listening to what the interviewee says and helping him or her to respond are the most important things to remember.

Speaking and Listening

> **summary**
> - Remember, for an interview to go well, planning the questions carefully is very important.
> - Be clear about what you want to find out.
> - Have a mixture of closed and open questions.
> - Think about how to put the interviewee at ease.

Questions

A

Look at the following questions. For each one say whether it is a closed question or an open one.

a) Where do you live?
b) Why do you think we should take global warming seriously?
c) What sort of things do you like to do at the weekend?
d) How many hours of television do you watch every week?
e) What do you think might be the best ways to warn young people about the dangers of drugs?

B

1. Why is it important to prepare your questions carefully before conducting an interview?
2. Name four things that might stop an interview going well. For each one say why it is a problem and how you can overcome it.
3. You have been asked to produce a leaflet entitled 'A Guide to Successful Interviewing for Young People'. Make the leaflet informative and attractive. Pay attention to the layout and design as well as the ideas and content.

C

You have been given the opportunity to interview a famous person of your choice. Decide who you will choose and prepare ten questions that you will ask the person. Imagine that the interview actually takes place. Write an account of what happens, including where it takes place, how you are feeling and how your famous guest answers your questions.

Group Work

Much of the work that you do in school requires you to cooperate in a group. Cooperating means working together, helping each other to understand and learn. You will have experience of working in many different types of groups, including small groups of two and three and much larger groups of 30 or more.

These pages are about working effectively in a group.

Why work in a group?

What do you think are some of the benefits of being able to work cooperatively in a group? Write down a list of ideas that come into your head.

Compare your list with the ideas below.

- Listening to different people's ideas helps you to understand more.
- Talking to other people helps to make things clearer in your mind.
- Working with different people makes you more flexible and adaptable.
- Taking part in a group helps your confidence.
- No one has all the right answers (not even the teacher!).
- Sharing ideas makes the most of everyone's individual skills and abilities.
- Working together can be more efficient and save time.
- Cooperation helps you to be responsible, preparing you for later life.

Of course we do not just work cooperatively in school. Everywhere in society — in the home, at work, playing sport or music — we work together with other people.

Sometimes we do need to work on our own, but a lot of the time cooperation with others is essential.

Imagine you are playing football or hockey and all the players decide to make up their own rules – the game could not go on. There would quickly be chaos. Or imagine you are singing in a choir or playing music in a group. What would happen if everyone started singing different songs or playing different tunes?

It is just the same when you are working in school, either with your whole class or in a smaller group. Everyone needs to be working together to help everyone get the best results.

How to work effectively in a group

If your teacher splits your class into groups and gives you all a task to perform, some groups will work better than others. Why is this? First of all think about groups that do not work well together. Can you suggest some reasons why a group might not cooperate effectively? The members of the group might not:

- **listen to each other**. As we have seen on pages 46–47, listening is very important in any discussion. After listening to different views on a subject you will understand it much more clearly.

Speaking and Listening

- **ask each other questions about the task.** You can help each other in a group by asking questions and encouraging everyone to share their opinions.
- **give each other the chance to speak and value everyone's ideas.** If everyone speaks at the same time, the result will be chaos. Everyone should be given the same chance to speak and listened to carefully. No one should put anyone else's ideas down.
- **help each other to come up with ideas.** Whenever you work as part of a group you share responsibility for that group. If the group is not working well together, it is up to all of the members to do something about it.

summary

- Cooperating in a group is an essential part of school and the outside world.
- Learning to work effectively in a group will improve your confidence and the quality of your work.
- You need to practise group work just as you need to practise your reading and writing.

Questions

A

1. What does 'to cooperate' mean?
2. List four reasons why it is a good idea to cooperate in a group. For each one give an example from your own experience to prove the point.

B

1. Think of three situations where it is important to work cooperatively in a group. Say what will happen if the group does not cooperate in each situation.
2. Why do people sometimes find it hard to work cooperatively? Suggest three practical ways to help people learn to be more cooperative. Design a poster aimed at encouraging cooperation.
3. Write a humorous description of a situation where people not working together causes chaos and confusion, for example, soldiers on a parade ground, workers on a production line, ballet dancers, an orchestra, etc.

C

Write the scripts for two short scenes showing the differences between two groups in the way they work together.

The groups are discussing the question, 'What is the point of homework?' One group works well together while one does not work cooperatively. Write the scenes like a playscript with four characters in each group.

51

Confidence in Front of an Audience

intro

At some time or another we all have to stand up and speak to an audience. It might be to read a story or a poem out loud. It might be to make a speech about an important issue or give a talk about a hobby. It might be connected with a piece of drama. Whatever the situation, confidence when speaking is very important and it is something you can practise and get better at.

> These pages are about learning to be confident when addressing an audience.

*I'm a really rotten reader
the worst in all the class,
the sort of rotten reader
that makes you want to laugh.*

from *Kingfisher Book of Common Verse* by Peter Dixon

Why is confidence important?

Look at these two openings to the same talk.

> 'What, er, I'd like to, er, talk about, is er, well, you know, er something I do in me er, spare time, you know, weekends and that, well not every weekend, but erm, well, you know what I mean, when I get the chance like, well, what I'm trying to say is ...'

> 'The thing I most like to do at weekends is go to the cinema. My favourite types of films are horror and comedy films. The funniest one I saw recently was ...'

It is easy to see which of these talks will be the most interesting to listen to. Being confident means you can put your ideas across in a clear and lively way so people will pay attention to what you have to say. Confidence will help you to be a better communicator.

Here are some key points to consider when speaking in front of an audience:
- **Intonation** – stress certain words and phrases to give them more importance (advertisers often stress words like new, low price, etc.).
- **Pauses** – you need to give your audience a chance to take in what you are saying.
- **Pace** – if you speak too quickly, no one will be able to understand you.
- **Clarity** – if your words are unclear, people will lose interest.
- **Eye contact** – always look at your audience to help get them involved.

Being prepared

The secret of being confident when speaking is good preparation. If you see politicians, for example, speaking on television, you will notice that they speak clearly and without much hesitation. This will be because they have practised what they want to say and will have learnt any important details they want to put across.

No one can speak confidently in front of an audience without a lot of practice; actors, for example, spend several weeks or months rehearsing their lines.

Reading out loud

Try reading the opening few lines to the following poem without any preparation.

Hiyamac.
Lobuddy.
Binearlong?
Cuplours.
Ketchanenny?
Goddafew.
Kindarthay?
Bassencarp.

from **Rods Poem** (Anon.)

The first time you read this it might not seem to make any sense. You would need to practise reading this poem several times before you could be confident of reading it with the correct American accent so that it makes sense.

What to prepare

Before you stand up in front of an audience you need to have planned what you are going to say. Whether you are reading a poem or story or you are giving a talk, the more you practise reading it out loud, the more confident you will feel.

summary

- The best way to become more confident when speaking in front of an audience is to plan carefully what you are going to say and to practise saying it out loud.

Questions

A

1. Why is it important to be confident when speaking in front of an audience?
2. Why is it a good idea to practise reading out loud?
3. Name three things that will improve a talk that you give to an audience.

B

1. Watch a person speaking on television, such as a newsreader, politician, actor, presenter. Make a list of five things he or she does to sound and look confident.
2. Someone you know has to give a talk in front of an audience. Prepare a checklist of ideas to help the person give the talk with confidence.

C

Prepare a talk about a subject that interests you. Make notes about how you are going to present the talk. Make a tape-recording of your talk, and note down ways in which you can improve your presentation so you will sound more confident.

53

Making a Persuasive Speech

intro

If you want to convince people that your idea on a particular subject is right, you will need to make a persuasive speech. This is a speech that persuades people to listen to you and to believe in you.

These pages are about how to make an effective persuasive speech.

Getting people on your side

As well as making your speech clear and easy to understand, you will have to try to use some other methods to get people on your side and to convince them that your ideas are worth listening to. Can you think of some ways to do this?

Some possibilities would be:
- tell a funny story at the beginning of your speech to get the audience on your side
- use pictures and other visual aids to make your speech more lively
- use facts and statistics to back up your argument
- ask the audience to think about certain questions that are important
- use persuasive language in your speech
- repeat certain key phrases that people can remember.

If you listen to politicians speaking, you will hear them use lots of these techniques.

How to persuade people

An example of a persuasive speech can be found in the following extract from the novel *Animal Farm* by the twentieth-century writer George Orwell. In the novel the animals on a farm have a revolution in which they rebel against their human masters and kick them off the farm. The revolution is started by an old pig called Major, who makes a powerful speech to the other animals persuading them to follow his ideas.

Persuasive techniques

Notice how in the extract Major directly addresses his audience, calling them 'comrades'. This makes his audience feel as if he is talking to them individually.

No animal in England knows the meaning of happiness or leisure after he is a year old. No animal in England is free. The life of an animal is misery and slavery: that is the plain truth.

But is this simply part of the order of Nature? Is it because this land of ours is so poor that it cannot afford a decent life to those who dwell upon it? No, comrades, a thousand times no! The soil of England is fertile, its climate is good, it is capable of affording food in abundance to an enormously greater number of animals than now inhabit it.

This single farm of ours would support a dozen horses, twenty cows, hundreds of sheep — and all of them living in a comfort and a dignity that are now almost beyond our imagining. Why then do we continue in this miserable condition? Because nearly the whole of the produce of our labour is stolen from us by human beings. There, comrades, is the answer to all our problems. It is summed up in a single word — Man. Man is the only real enemy we have. Remove Man from the scene, and the root cause of hunger and overwork is abolished for ever.

Man is the only creature that consumes without producing. He does not give milk, he does not lay eggs, he is too weak to pull the plough, he cannot run fast enough to catch rabbits. Yet he is lord of all the animals. He sets them to work, he gives back to them the bare minimum that will prevent them from starving, and the rest he keeps for himself.

from *Animal Farm* by George Orwell

Speaking and Listening

When you make a persuasive speech it is very important to talk directly to your audience all the time and involve them in your ideas.

After you have prepared the ideas for your speech you need to decide how you can involve your audience and get them on your side. Asking the audience questions is a very good way of doing this because it makes them think about what you are saying. Another effective technique is to make short statements that can be easily understood and remembered, such as 'Man is the only real enemy we have'.

summary

- To make a persuasive speech you need to involve the audience in what you are saying.
- Your ideas need to be clear and easy to understand.
- You need to back up you ideas with evidence or statistics to show that what you are saying is right.

Questions

A

1. Why might you tell a funny story at the beginning of a persuasive speech?
2. Why are facts and statistics important in persuasive speeches?
3. Why might you want to ask your audience questions when making a persuasive speech?
4. How can you help your audience to remember your ideas?
5. Name a group of people who often make persuasive speeches in society.

B

1. In the extract from *Animal Farm* what evidence does Major use to make his point?
2. Pick out three statements from his speech that are clear and persuasive. For each one explain in your own words the point he is making.
3. Do you think the speech will work to persuade his audience to do something about their situation?
4. Prepare a reading of this speech as if you were addressing a real audience. You will need to decide which words and phrases to emphasise, where to pause, where to speak quietly, etc.

C

1. Write a speech that the farmer would make to the animals in answer to Major's speech. He will need to persuade the animals that Major is wrong and that life on the farm is wonderful.
2. Write your own persuasive speech about a subject you are interested in. Remember, the point of your speech is to persuade your audience to believe your ideas.
   - Some suggestions might be:
   Smoking should be banned in all public places.
   All schools should be single sex.
   There should be more sports and practical activities in school.

F

Although *Animal Farm* might seem to be written for children, with talking animals, it is really about what can happen when people start a revolution in society. George Orwell cleverly based the events of the book on a real historical event, the Russian Revolution of 1917.

55

Skimming, Scanning and Close Reading

These pages are about different ways of reading for different purposes.

intro

You do not always need to read every detail in every text you see. Sometimes all you need is to get a general idea of what a text is about, especially when you are reading to find out information. In this situation, a quicker method of reading is better than one which pays close attention to every single word.

Skimming and scanning

When you read information texts to research a topic, you want to answer some questions quickly. Does the book have details about the topic? Which pages will be useful? Will you be able to find enough of the facts to answer your questions?

Skimming is a very quick method of reading to get the general idea (the gist) of a text. You might skim-read the list of **contents** (the chapters or sections listed at the front of the book) or the **index** (the alphabetical list of topics covered in the book, found at the back).

Changing Minds – Britain 15

Your enquiries

Life and death

1. **Dead and gone**
   How can we learn about hidden lives? — 6

2. **'So famous a city'**
   What was fine and what was foul in London life? — 14

3. **Vagrants and vagabonds**
   Did life change for the beggars of Bristol? — 24

4. **A woman's life**
   How can historians disagree when they are working with the ...urces? — 32

Into the pit

Your friend has a surprise for you. It is a dry day so the open-air theatres on the south bank of the river will be putting on plays. There is to be a new play by William Shakespeare at the Globe Theatre. This is exciting news. You have heard how fine the English theatre is.

Your brother points out a flag that is flying high above the theatre. This means a play will soon begin. You join a crowd heading towards the theatre entrance. Your English friend advises you to hold tightly onto the purse that hangs from your belt. **Cutpurses** mingle in these crowds and they can slice off a purse without you feeling a thing.

Finally you reach the theatre. You pay to sit high in a gallery. Down below the poorest people are standing by the stage. The area they are standing in is called the pit. They look a pretty rough lot, but the people sitting near you are well-dressed and polite.

The play begins. It is called 'Macbeth'. There are moments of great poetry and moments of great comedy. There is much cheering and jeering at the actors – especially at the women, who are played by young boys. Everyone feels a strange thrill when witches or ghosts appear on stage. There is a battle scene near the end when animal blood is splashed all over those nearest the stage!

As you leave the theatre a fight breaks out. It grows into a small riot and your friend hurries you away. He explains that this often happens when large crowds gather and there is too much drinking. Strict church-goers, called **Puritans**, want the theatre to be banned.

20

Study Skills

Then you would **skim-read** the pages listed in the index to get the gist of information there, and see how clearly presented it is.

Skim read the extracts on these pages, and the **B** questions below. Have you got the gist of topics you will answer questions about?

Scanning is a way of reading when you are looking for specific information. It is quick because you do not read each word carefully. Instead, you look down the page for key words, then you just read those short sections to find out what you need to know.

Close reading

When you have found the information you want to understand thoroughly, you will be looking for more than just the facts. **Close reading** is when you read every word and think about what you read.

Republic, The   2, 84, 86
Roman Catholics   50, 51, 54, 57, 66, 68, 73, 80, 93, 94, 95, 96, 97, 98, 100
Roundheads   64–73, 75 76, 77
Royal Society   118–25
Royalists   64–73, 75, 76, 79

science   5, 118–25
Scotland   40–7, 59, 68, 75, 78, 89, 96, 113
Shakespeare   20–21
Ship Money   69, 71, 73
Spanish Armada   2, 56, 60, 61

taxes   27, 28, 50, 62, 66, 68, 71, 81, 88
theatre   20–21
trade   7, 14–23, 52, 62, 69, 73, 75, 103, 107, 108

vagrants and vagabonds   24–31

from *Changing Minds*
by Byrom, Counsell, Riley and Stephens-Wood

You will form opinions which show understanding of the ideas in what you have read. You will also be able to give reasons for your opinions, based on evidence you can point out.

summary

- **Skimming:** this is speed reading to get the general idea.
- **Scanning:** this is speed reading to find specific facts.
- **Close reading:** this is reading carefully to form opinions about the facts.

Questions

A

1. What is skimming? When is it a useful method of reading?
2. What is scanning, and when would you use this method of reading?
3. What kind of information will you find when you skim and scan? What extra understanding will you gain from close reading?
4. Would you skim, scan or close read if you were:
   a) looking at a review to decide if you will buy a new video
   b) looking for today's TV guide in a newspaper or magazine
   c) looking for names of goal scorers in a football match report?

B

1. Skim-read the extracts from the contents page and index. From memory, make a list of topics included in this book.
2. Scan the description of the visit to the Globe Theatre. Write down four facts you learn about the theatre building. Write down three facts you learn about the play.
3. Close read the description 'Into the pit', then write a detailed explanation of the reasons why a visit to the Globe Theatre was somewhat risky, but very entertaining.

C

Practise the reading skills you have learnt about on these pages by finding two more books which give information about the Globe Theatre. Imagine you are a Puritan. Write a letter, explaining the reasons you disapprove of theatre-going so strongly.

For more information on reading and researching see pages 58–59

Using the Library

These pages are about how libraries are organised.

intro

The word library has its roots in the Latin word for a book **liber**, although nowadays you will find much more than books in the library in your school or neighbourhood.

How many different sources of information can you see here?

However, books still take up most of the space on library shelves. To find the books containing the information you are searching for, you need to understand how libraries organise their collections of books.

Fiction or non-fiction?

The first thing you need to know is the difference between **fiction** and **non-fiction**. In most libraries, books are divided into these two categories and kept in different places. The two types of book are organised on the shelves using different systems.

Fiction books (novels and stories) are usually organised in alphabetical order of their authors' surnames. You would find books by Roald Dahl near the beginning of the fiction shelves and books by Robert Westall near the end. Some libraries have a separate section for teenage fiction.

Non-fiction books include reference books like **encyclopedias** and **dictionaries**, and factual books about different subjects. In most school and local libraries these are organised by a method called the Dewey System which divides books into ten main groups or classes according to what subject they are about. Each group has a number as follows:

    000   Reference books
    100   Philosophy
    200   Religion
    300   Social Sciences (law, politics, careers, etc.)
    400   Languages
    500   Maths and Pure Science (physics, biology)
    600   Applied Science (medicine, engineering)
    700   Arts and Hobbies
    800   Literature
    900   History, Biography and Geography

Because there are ten classes, this is sometimes called the **Dewey Decimal System**. Each of the ten classes is divided up into more precise subjects. For example, Social Science classifications include the following:

    331   Careers
    346   Law
    355   The armed forces
    370   Education
    380   Transport

The way the classes of books are split up into specific topics looks just like decimal numbers. If you look at the shelf holding books on transport, you find they are classified like this:

    385.09   Railways
    386.46   Canals
    388.428   London Underground
    388.460   Trams

So, the more precise the classification, the more numbers you will see after the decimal point.

Study Skills

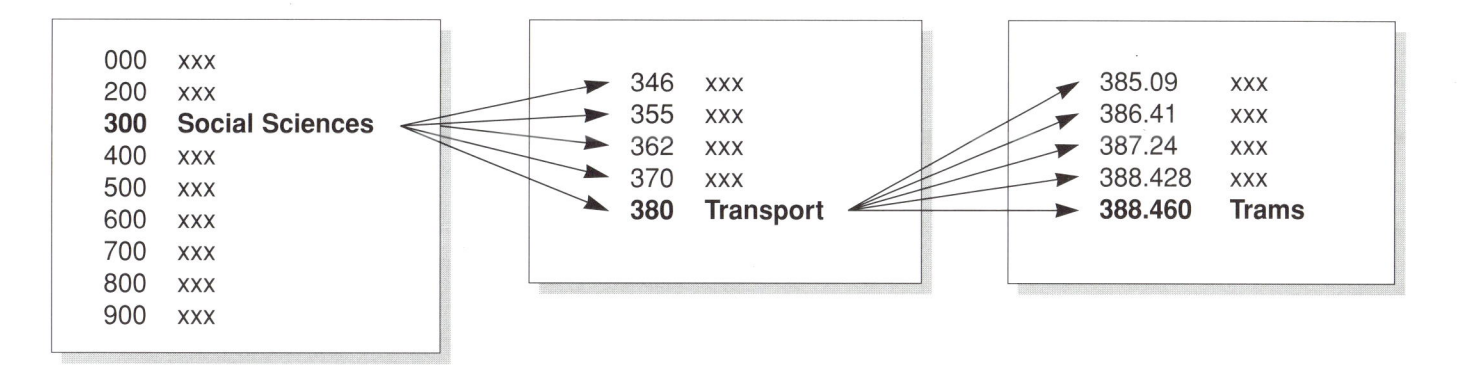

000	xxx
200	xxx
300	**Social Sciences**
400	xxx
500	xxx
600	xxx
700	xxx
800	xxx
900	xxx

346	xxx
355	xxx
362	xxx
370	xxx
380	**Transport**

385.09	xxx
386.41	xxx
387.24	xxx
388.428	xxx
388.460	**Trams**

Catalogues – and how to use them

In every library there is a subject index where topics are listed in alphabetical order. This index will tell you which Dewey numbers classify books with information about each topic. Here are some extracts from one topic listed:

Animals	conservation	639.9
	cruelty to	179.3
	medical experiments	619
	pets	636.0887

On the library computer, the books will be catalogued in a number of different ways which will help you find what you are looking for:

- If you know the Dewey number for a topic, you can find out every book the library has with that classification.
- Book titles are also listed, so you can enter a key word and the computer will list all the titles including that word.
- Or, if you know who wrote a particular book, you can look up the author's name.

summary

Libraries classify books differently depending if they are fiction or non-fiction:
- **Non-fiction books are grouped according to their subjects, numbered according to the Dewey System. There are ten main classes in the Dewey System, each divided into many smaller categories. You can find out the Dewey classification number of a topic by looking it up in the subject index.**
- **Fiction books are shelved in alphabetical order of author's names.**
- **Don't forget that modern libraries have information in many formats, not just books.**

Questions

A

1. What is the origin of the word library?
2. List five different sources of information that you might find in a modern library.
3. How many main groups are there in the Dewey system?
4. If you wanted a book on animal rights, which classification number would you look for?
5. If you wanted a biography, which section of the library would you go to?

B

1. Draw a plan of your school library or local library showing where different books are shelved as well as other items like videos, tapes, CDs and magazines.
2. Make a leaflet suitable for a 9–10-year-old explaining how the Dewey System works.
3. Write a short illustrated guidebook to your school or local library, suitable for someone just starting Key Stage 3 work. Explain what can be found in the library and how to find it.

C

Pay a visit to your school or local library and spend some time making sure you are able to make use of the subject index and the catalogue system. How quickly can you locate a particular book on the shelves?

For more information about research see pages 60–61

Research from Information Texts

These pages are about how to research a topic, identifying and putting together information from a variety of different sources.

intro

There will be many times when you will be told to 'go away and find out' about a topic. To do this task well, you need to remember the following:

- To get the best available information, use more than one source – books, videos, magazines, etc.
- Know in advance what kind of information you are looking for – have some questions in your head, or better still written down on paper.
- Make notes about what you find out – and where from – so you can go back to your source if you need more detail later on.

Possible sources of information

Encyclopedia
✓ Easy to find in any library.
✓ Easy to look up relevant information.
✓ Will give you some information.
✗ It might be out of date.
✗ It might be hard to understand.
✗ It might be less detailed than you need.

CD-ROM encyclopedia
✓ Probably available in school.
✓ Easy to look up and to print information and pictures.
✓ Should be quite up to date.
✗ It might be focused on North America rather than Europe.
✗ It might be hard to understand.
✗ It might be less detailed than you need.

Non-fiction books
✓ Provide a wide variety of information.
✓ Some will be easier to understand than an encyclopedia.
✗ Hard to identify the best books to use.
✗ Library books might be out on loan.
✗ More difficult to find the exact information you need.

Newspapers/magazines/teletext
✓ Easily available – even at home.
✓ Up to date.
✗ Information limited to what is 'in the news'.
✗ Not always possible to find the information you need.
✗ Information may be biased.

CD-ROM newspapers
✓ Probably available in school.
✓ Information from several years' news.
✓ Easy to find the topic you are researching.
✗ Might not provide the exact information you need.
✗ Might be hard to understand.

Leaflets and booklets from charities and campaigning organisations
✓ Easily available.
✓ Cheap.
✓ Easy to read.
✗ You might have to wait several days if you have to write off for these.
✗ Information might be biased.

Television/video, radio/tapes
✓ Easily available – even at home.
✓ Interesting and easy to watch/listen to.
✓ Probably up to date (though check dates on videos).
✗ Might not be broadcast live when you need it.
✗ More difficult to make notes than from written sources of information.

The Internet
✓ Information is up to date.
✓ Easy to print off information and pictures.
✗ Might be difficult to get to use it.
✗ Can be expensive if you're paying.
✗ Not always easy to find the exact information you are looking for.

Study Skills

Collecting information from a variety of sources

A useful method for gathering together the relevant facts from a range of different sources is the **project grid**. On a large sheet of paper (A3, or even bigger, if you can find it) prepare some questions you want to answer and list them on the left-hand side of the page.

As you look up information from different sources, put the titles and authors along the top of the grid. Make a note of facts you discover – and the page numbers, if it was from a long book – in the appropriate space on the grid. Here is an example, notice how two sources provided no information for the first question.

Research about endangered species: the giant panda

	Children's encyclopedia	CD-ROM encyclopedia	Book – *Pandas* by Jane Goodall	Worldwide Fund for Nature leaflet	CD-ROM newspapers	TV documentary
What is causing their numbers to fall?	People clear bamboo to grow crops. Pandas eat 10–20 kg daily		Every 20–100 yrs, bamboo flowers and dies – then pandas starve	Bamboo forest died back – 1000 pandas in 1983, now only about 300	Hard to breed in captivity, e.g. Chichi in London Zoo	
In which countries do Pandas live?						

summary

- When you need to find information, remember that there are many different sources: books; media texts, like newspapers and television; information technology, like CD-ROMS; the Internet. Decide which will be most suitable for your topic.
- Note down the sources you use and the information you discover.
- A project grid may help you collect facts from several different sources.

Questions

A

Which would be the best sources of information about each of the topics below? Why?

a) Acid rain – what causes it, why it is a problem.
b) Life in a monastery during the Middle Ages.
c) Films released this week.
d) The life and writings of Charles Dickens.
e) Opinions about foxhunting in Britain.

B

1 Choose a television or radio programme which looks as if it will provide information about a topic you want to research. Before you watch or listen, write down five questions about the topic. Make notes about information you discover which answers your questions.

2 Choose an animal or plant which is in danger of extinction. Make a project grid with room to make notes on five sources of information and at least five of your own questions. Complete your grid, finding information from books, media texts and information technology texts, if possible.

3 Choose one of the topics listed in **A**. Make and complete a project grid about the topic consulting as wide a range of sources of information as you are able.

C

Choose a topic to research (you may already have a project to do for English, or another subject, at school). Make a project grid listing at least ten questions you want to answer. Complete the grid with information from a wide variety of sources. Write up your project, making full use of the information noted down on your grid.

For more information about research skills see pages 58–59 and 62–63

Making Notes and Summaries

intro

Notes and summaries are brief ways of writing things down, either for your own use, or to pass on information and ideas in a concise form.

These pages are about why you need to make notes and summaries of information and different ways of note making.

When do I need to make notes?

Being able to make good, concise notes will often be useful in school. For example:

- Your teacher is talking, and you want to remember important points.
- You are reading a text and you want to write down your ideas about it.
- You are researching information for a project.
- You are planning a piece of writing.
- You are revising for an exam.

From these examples you will see that notes have two main purposes:

- Notes can help you to make sense of information.
- Notes can help you to remember information.

Lists

When revising for an exam, or listening to a teacher talk in a lesson, a list might be the best way for you to make notes. Pick out key words. Use them as headings. Underline them. Number them. Connect other main ideas with them.

Make the list as brief as you possibly can, so you can learn it.

Here are some extracts from a book about classical mythology. Read the extracts and make a list of the key points.

ZEUS (Jupiter, Jove) was the king of earth and air and overlord of Olympus, yet even he was not wholly free from the power of Fate. He figures as a magnificent form, white-haired and bearded, sometimes crowned with oak leaves, holding in his hands the thunderbolts with which he scourged impiety. An eagle attends him as minister of his will and for page or cup-bearer he has Ganymede, a boy so beautiful that Zeus had him stolen from Mount Ida to make him immortal in heaven.

HERA (Juno) wife of Zeus, was the legitimate queen of Olympus. Through her jealousy she led her husband a troubled life. Her other characteristics were pride and self-satisfaction and always she proved quick to take offence at any slight on the part of gods or men. Her handmaid was Iris, the rainbow, who carried her messages to earth. Her daughter Hebe served with Ganymede as cup-bearer at the celestial table.

APOLLO (with Phoebus prominent among his many aliases) was the most beautiful and the most beloved of the Olympians. Beside his sister Selene, the moon, he figures as Helios, the sun, and was sometimes also known as Hyperion. He was the son of Zeus and Leto (Latona) who was driven to Delos by the jealousy of Hera (Juno). Because of Hera's continuing persecution of his mother, Apollo was reared by Themis, and thrived so well in this setting that at his first taste of nectar and ambrosia he burst his swaddling-clothes and stood forth a fully-grown youth, demanding the lyre and silver bow with which he is usually represented.

ARTEMIS (Diana), Apollo's twin sister, also had several aliases. One was the renowned Diana of the Ephesians, whose temple ranked among the Seven Wonders; another was the cruel goddess Tauris. The Arcadian Artemis was a goddess of hunting and wildlife. She was chaste to a fault and her fatal jealousy was more easily aroused not by love, but by presumption on the part of mortals.

from *Classical Guide to Mythology* by R.R. Hope

Study Skills

Topic webs

For some people, a list of words is hard to remember. It is not very interesting to look at! You can make notes that use colours and pictures to emphasise key words. These can be good for sorting out ideas before you write an essay, or as you put together a plan for a project, or a way of summarising all the important information to revise for a test or exam.

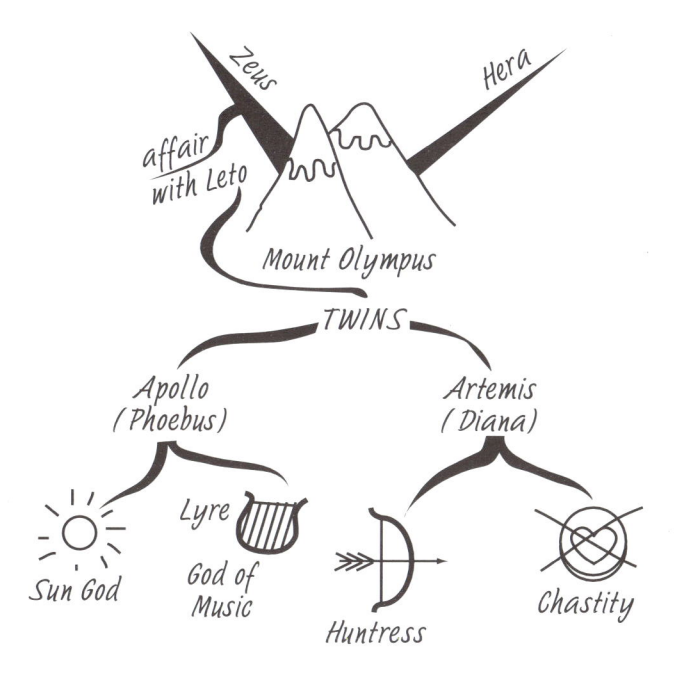

summary

- Notes can help you make sense of what you read, or what you are told.
- Notes can help you remember information.
- Notes summarise information.
- Good notes are selective – don't highlight or write down too much.
- Good notes are not just copied out – use your own words.
- Summaries are like notes because they focus on key points and essential information.

Summary writing

Notes are usually just for yourself, to help you with ideas or to jog your memory, but a summary may be for someone else, so it needs to be written in sentences.

To summarise a piece of writing, start off by making notes about the key points, then put the main ideas into your own words. Miss out description and any background information.

For example, the following summary is 55 words – about a third of the original length of the descriptions of Apollo and Artemis.

Apollo and Artemis were twin brother and sister. Their father was Zeus, their mother was a woman called Leto. Apollo is often pictured holding a lyre to show he was a musician. He is also the sun-god. Artemis is the goddess of hunting and wildlife. She chose to live a life without men's love.

Questions

A

1. What are the two main reasons for making notes?
2. Which method of making notes would you choose, and why, for:
   a) gathering together ideas for a story
   b) making sense of a difficult poem
   c) revising for a test or examination.
3. Explain two differences between bad notes and good notes.
4. How can good notes help you write a summary?

B

1. Draw your own topic web. Add information about Zeus and Hera, Use sketches and colours to help you remember details.
2. List all the names mentioned in the extract about Zeus, Hera, Apollo and Artemis. Note down one fact about each, e.g. Ganymede – servant of Zeus.
3. Write a 50-word summary of the most important information given above about the King and Queen of Olympus, Zeus and Hera.

C

Do some research and add to your notes by finding out more about these other gods and goddesses of Greece – Athene (Minerva), Ares (Mars), Hermes (Mercury), Aphrodite (Venus), Eros (Cupid), Posidon (Neptune) and Hephaestus (Vulcan). The names in brackets are the Roman names. Some of them may be more familiar to you than the Greek names.

For more information about making notes see pages 60–61

Charts, Graphs and Tables

Pictures really can be worth a thousand words when you are explaining some kinds of information. Below are some different kinds of visual displays of information, including graphs, diagrams and tables, for you to interpret.

These pages are about different ways information can be presented visually.

Every year, about two hundred 11-year-olds join Year 7 at Greenfields School. They mostly come from seven junior schools. The biggest school is West Park Primary School, which is in town, quite near Greenfields. St Paul's is nearby and most Year 6 children from there move to Greenfields. Cherry Tree and Dane Street are on the other side of town, but some children choose to travel from there to Greenfields. The smallest schools are in three villages, Redling, Lowdale and Littleham, all two to three miles out of town. Almost all the Year 6 children from these villages go to Greenfields.

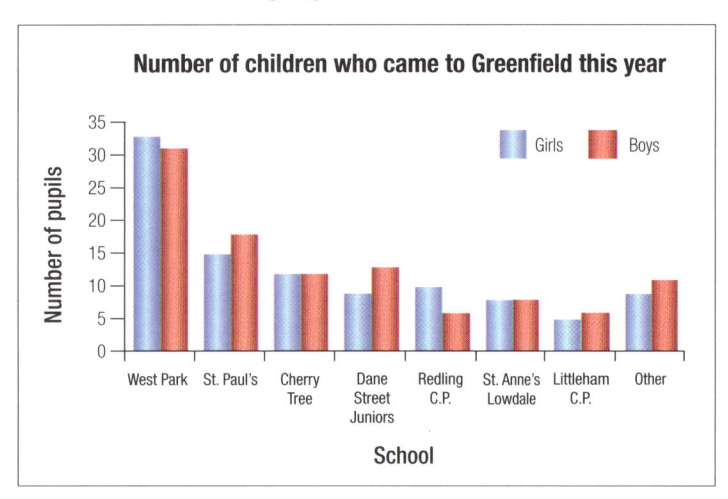

Bar graph

This graph shows several pieces of information, including:

- which primary schools send children to Greenfields
- how many children come from each primary school
- how many girls and how many boys come from each primary school
- how many boys and how many girls there will be altogether in Year 7.

Pie chart

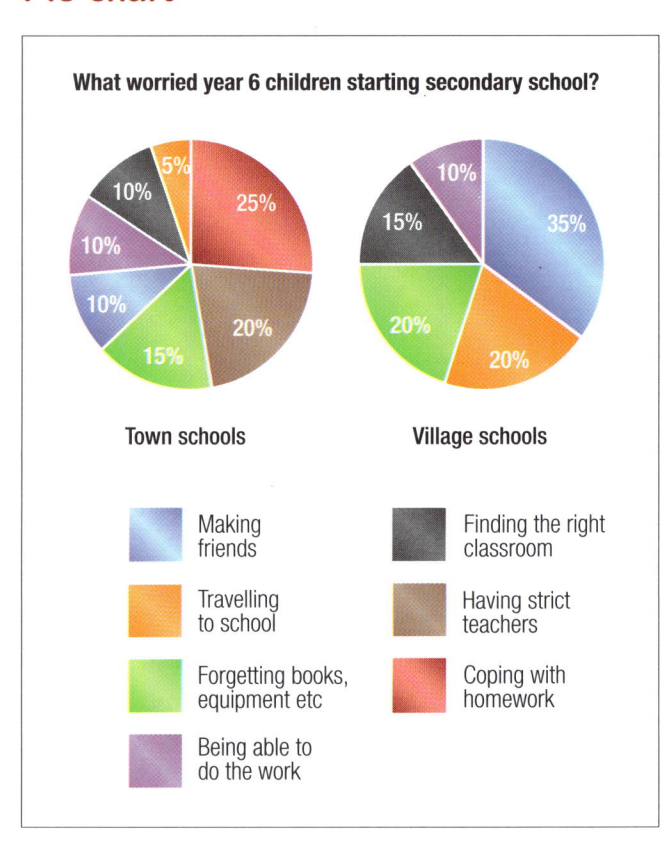

What worried year 6 children starting secondary school?

Town schools / Village schools

- Making friends
- Travelling to school
- Forgetting books, equipment etc
- Being able to do the work
- Finding the right classroom
- Having strict teachers
- Coping with homework

These charts give you information about:

- things that worried Year 6 children about starting at Greenfields
- the percentage of children who identified particular major worries
- the differences between worries of children from the town primary schools compared with children from the village schools.

64

Basic Information Texts

Table

This is part of the timetable for everyone in Year 7. It gives information about what subjects pupils have from Monday to Wednesday. If you look at it you can see the classrooms where Year 7 will be during lessons and where the pupils will move around the school between lessons.

	REGISTRATION			BREAK		LUNCH		
Monday		Science G2	Languages S14		Humanities M4		Technology G20	Maths S1
Tuesday		Art/Music/Drama Arts Block	English M18		Technology G20		Languages S14	Science G2
Wednesday		Maths (I.T) Sixth Form Block	Humanities M4		Tutor Time G2		Games Sports Hall	English M18

summary

- Visual displays are good for giving you information at a glance. They can summarise facts and figures. They can show you things like times, for example a train timetable, and places, for example a map of the city centre.
- If you look at different types of display relating to the same topic, one can sometimes help you get more information from another.
- But visual displays cannot explain reasons, causes and consequences. You need words to do that.

Questions

A

1. What kind of information can visual displays show more easily than words?
2. Are there more boys or girls in Year 7?
3. What worries the largest percentage of children from the town schools? What worries the largest percentage of children from the village schools?
4. What worries town children but not village children?

B

1. At the end of break on the first Tuesday of term, you find a new Year 7 pupil looking worried near the Year 7 office. The pupil tells you that she is not sure where to go for the next lesson, and does not know what equipment will be needed. Look at the timetable and write down what you would say to help this pupil.

2. Write an information sheet to help the new Year 7 pupils during their first few weeks in the school. You could include a letter welcoming them to Greenfields and a section on 'Your questions answered' with reassurance about common worries.

C

Write an information sheet to help the new Year 7 pupils at your own school.

For more information on visual presentation see pages 68–69

Writing Instructions

> These pages are about how to present written information clearly and logically.

intro

Many things we buy come with instructions. Some are quite straightforward like the directions for use on shampoo. Some are more complicated like the manual you get with a new computer. It is easy to tell good instructions from bad ones – Good instructions are organised, clear and easy to follow.

What are good instructions?

Which of the sets of instructions below would you find easier to follow?
How does the way they are set out – and the way they are worded – make a difference?

YOUR NEW VIDEO – SETTING THE CLOCK:

1. Press the '**program**' button on the remote control.
2. Press **no. 1** to choose to set the clock.
3. Enter the correct date using the '**change channel**' button and press '**select**'.
4. Enter the correct **month** (number) as above.
5. Enter the **hour** (24 hour clock) as above.
6. Enter the **correct minutes** as above.
7. The picture, with correct date and time will be displayed on the screen.

PROGRAMING TO TAPE FROM THE TELEVISION:

1. Press '**program**' button on remote control.
2. Press **no. 2** to select '**program**' from on-screen menu ...

Dear Jo

You asked me to write and tell you how to program this new video you just bought. Well, don't ask me, I'm hopeless with machines, but I'll tell you what you do with the one I've got.

First you have to press something on the remote control, but before that, put a tape in the machine. It's a button that says program.

Then a list comes up on the screen, only I can't remember all of that, but you press number 2 (I think!) on the remote thingy, unless it says clock. If that's on the list, you have to put the right time in somehow. Once you've done that, then you can press 2 ...

Diagrams and flow charts

Sometimes a diagram will help to make instructions clear.

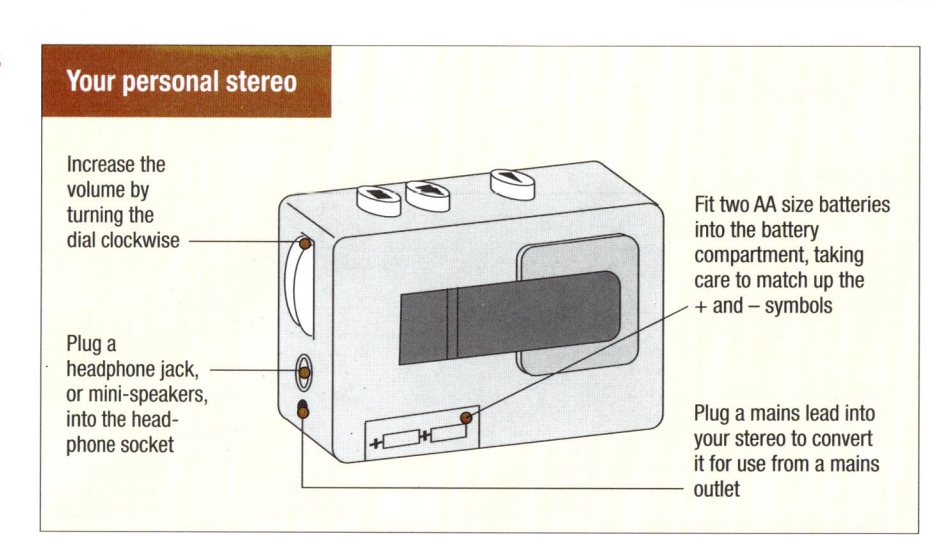

Your personal stereo

- Increase the volume by turning the dial clockwise
- Plug a headphone jack, or mini-speakers, into the headphone socket
- Fit two AA size batteries into the battery compartment, taking care to match up the + and − symbols
- Plug a mains lead into your stereo to convert it for use from a mains outlet

Basic Information Texts

It may be easier to give complex instructions in the form of a **flow chart**. Flow charts are useful if you are showing how to solve a problem. If one solution does not work, a flow chart can show quickly and clearly what to try next.

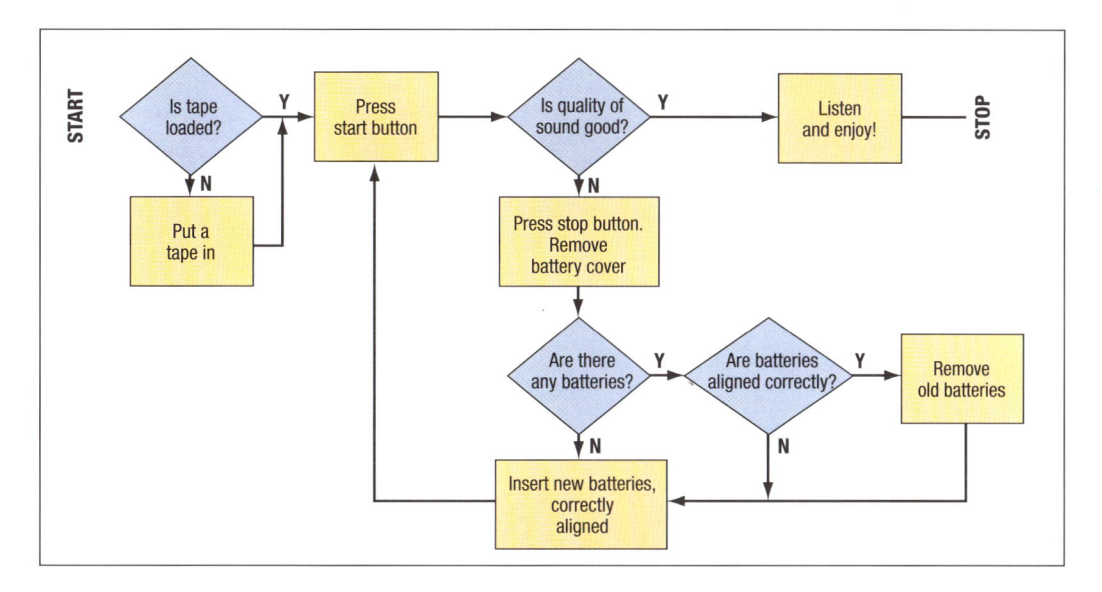

```
START → [Is tape loaded?] --Y--> [Press start button] → [Is quality of sound good?] --Y--> [Listen and enjoy!] → STOP
              |N                                              |N
              ↓                                               ↓
         [Put a tape in]                          [Press stop button. Remove battery cover]
                                                              ↓
                                                  [Are there any batteries?] --Y--> [Are batteries aligned correctly?] --Y--> [Remove old batteries]
                                                              |N                                  |N
                                                              ↓                                   ↓
                                                  [Insert new batteries, correctly aligned]
```

Summary

Good instructions:
- have a short, clear title
- give precise, short, step-by-step details.
- Usually each instruction is a command – it starts with a verb such as put, press, etc.
- Diagrams may be included.
- Flow charts can give complicated instructions as they can show alternative possible actions.

Questions

A

1. Pick out three particularly confusing bits from the bad set of instructions. Briefly, explain why each of the bits you chose would be hard to follow.
2. Now pick out the words which explain the same three 'confusing bits' in the second set of instructions. What features of 'good' instructions can you spot in these examples?
3. Why might a diagram help you to follow instructions more easily?
4. What kind of instructions are most clearly explained on a flow chart?

B

1. Design a leaflet to go with the personal stereo. Include a diagram of the front as well as the back. Number the labels and write a list of instructions to explain how to make the stereo work.
2. Use the flow chart to help you write a list of detailed instructions, with diagrams, to show how to replace old batteries.
3. Does someone in your family need help with something you are an expert on?

   Make a four-page instruction manual (fold a sheet of A4 paper in half) giving clear organised guidance.

   It could be about: how to look cool; how to tidy your bedroom; how to look clean and smart; how to play a game; how to cook something; how to make something work.

C

Practise giving clear spoken instructions to a member of your family or a friend. Give instructions – words only, no demonstrations – about how to perform an unfamiliar task such as sewing on a button, wiring a plug, writing and sending an e-mail letter. Can your partner follow your instructions correctly?

For more information about presenting information using diagrams see pages 64–65

Texts Combining Words and Pictures

These pages are about how words and pictures can be combined to organise and present information in an interesting way.

intro

Whether it's a poster, a newspaper story, an advertisement or an encyclopedia entry, writers use many techniques to make information easier to read and understand.

Here is the first draft of a wall poster. It aims to give young people practical advice about different ways to care for the environment. Study the poster design and the notes giving suggestions for improvements.

Good, clear heading. Use green for frame to poster?

Facts in red (for danger).

Picture of earth is good. Emphasise green and blue colours – make it look alive!

Good idea – use red for wrong, green for right?

Bullet points?

Eight ways to go green

7 – Say no to plastic bags
Plastic is hard to recycle, so avoid buying things in unnecessary plastic packaging. Reuse carrier bags, or better still, take a durable bag when you go shopping.

1 – Recycle waste
90% of our waste ends up on rubbish tips. Do your bit to help – find out where your local recycling centre is. Put glass in the bottle bank. Cans – wash them out and put them in a can bank. Paper – put your newspapers in the paper bank. Plastic containers – if you don't have a collection point yet, write to your local authority and ask for one.

FACT 1 – The average family in Britain throws away ONE TONNE of rubbish a year.

8 – Shop green
DON'T BUY
Aerosols – they damage the ozone layer, and that's dangerous for our skins. Don't use products which con[tain] CFCs. Products which destroy the rainforest. Trees cre[ate] oxygen. They are homes to many species of wildlife. [They] protect the soil. Food from animals kept in unnatural surroundings, like eggs from battery hens.

2 – Care for the countryside
WRONG
✗ Rubbish left behind can hurt animals and pollute rivers.
✗ Gates left open can hurt livestock.
✗ Walking across fields can damage crops.
RIGHT
✓ Fasten all gates.
✓ Keep dogs under control.
✓ Take your litter home.
✓ Stick to the footpaths.
✓ Follow the Country Code.

FACT 2 – a 1% reduction in room temperature can lower heating bills by 10%.

3 – Save water
It might always seem to be raining, but British rivers and reservoirs are drying up. You can save water by: using the shower, not the bath making sure taps are properly turned off using a watering can in the garden and a bucket to clean the car, not a hose.

68

Basic Information Texts

Making the facts clear

To get the message across effectively, a writer may need to make choices about:

- **layout** – the overall design of the text
- **headings and subheadings** – where, and how worded
- **typeface** (also called **font**) – size, style and colour
- **illustrations** – use of photos, drawings, cartoons, and the written captions that go with them
- **wording** – choosing between continuous sentences or lists, questions and answers.

Needs some pictures showing how to do it right. Find photos to fill in spaces, e.g. 'green' cleaning products; beautiful countryside; recycling centres etc.

6 – Shop green
DO BUY
Products which are good for the environment, like recyled kitchen paper, unbleached disposable nappies, detergent-free washing liquids, pump action or roll-on deodorants, organic foods, ie meat and vegetables produced without chemicals. Cosmetics which aren't tested on animals and tuna fish that is caught by methods that don't harm dolphins.

FACT 3 – A mile of motorway uses up 25 acres of land.

5 – Leave the car at home
Cars pollute the atmosphere. Building more roads destroys the countryside. Instead of driving you can walk, use a bike or public transport.

Great list!

FACT 4 – Some CFCs stay in the atmosphere for 100 years.

– Save energy
...and electricity production uses up fossil fuels and ...ages the atmosphere. SAVE IT.
...urn off lights, etc., when you leave the room.
...urn down the cental heating thermostat.
...ake sure your washing machine has a full load.
...oil just the water you need in the kettle.
...ry washing outside when it's fine.

Include an address for further information here, e.g Friends of the Earth

Needs bullet points. Could be right and wrong – like 2.

For more information about visual presentation of information see pages 64–65 and 66–67

---

summary

- To present information well, think about: layout, headings, typeface, illustrations and wording.

Questions

A

1. Why would green and red be good colours to choose for some of the writing on the wall poster?
2. Why is the background picture of the Earth effective?
3. Why would it improve the leaflet if photographs were added to the poster?
4. Which boxes present information in the clearest way?
5. Which two boxes are least clear to read, and how could they be improved?

B

1. Rewrite the information in boxes 1, 3, 6 and 8, following the advice in the notes on the poster.
2. Find three or four suitable photos, for example from magazine adverts or catalogues, to complete the poster. Write captions for these illustrations, following the advice from the notes on the poster.
3. Produce an improved draft of this poster, taking notice of the suggestions marked around it.

C

Think of another topic which would be of interest to a friend or someone in your family. Make a wall poster about the topic. Here are some ideas:

- keeping a pet (cat, dog, tropical fish, or something more unusual)
- the history of an interesting place near where you live
- the players and recent games of a favourite sports team
- new computer games/software
- classic cars/motorcycles.

Writing a Report

> These pages are about how to express yourself clearly when you are passing on written information in a formal report.

intro

A report is another way of passing on information. The term report is given to several different types of writing, but what they have in common is that they gather together and sum up information about a particular subject – as your end of year school report does about your progress. A report comes to conclusions and may be read by many people.

There are four steps to writing a report. You have to:

- **research** – collect together evidence from looking around you, talking to people about their experiences, reading about other research similar to yours
- **evaluate** – study the evidence you have collected and draw some conclusions about what it means
- **write** – describe the evidence you have collected and explain the conclusions you have drawn and your reasons for them
- **recommend** – sum up what action you think needs to be taken in the future, based on your conclusions.

Organising your report

A report is usually organised into several sections. These are explained on the left side of the extracts shown below. The style of writing you need to use is explained on the right side of the extracts.

The title

> SCHOOL UNIFORM PROPOSALS
> – the debate and some suggestions,
> based on an investigation by Year 8

Factual and to the point – makes it clear exactly what is in this report

Terms of reference

> ### Terms of reference
> 1. To present Year 8's opinions about proposed changes to our school uniform to Year Council and to parents.
> 2. To consider advantages and disadvantages of the two options, modern and traditional, suggested by parents.
> 3. To propose Year 8's suggestions for changes to the school uniform.

A list sets out:
- *who the report is for*
- *an outline of information in it*
- *where information has been collected.*

Findings
This is the longest section. Here is the introduction:

> ### Why have a school uniform?
> There are many reasons why schools choose to have a uniform. In some schools, there will be a wide range of pupils, some with affluent backgrounds than others, and a uniform not only looks smart and shows which school pupils belong to, it also makes all pupils equal.
>
> A survey of the opinions of pupils in Year 8 was carried out and it was discovered that …

Style is impersonal – strictly third person.

This uses the passive voice '… it was discovered that …' so words like I and we are avoided.

Vocabulary is very formal (e.g. affluent). Standard English is essential.

70

Basic Information Texts

Here is the start of another section of the findings:

Traditional v. modern option
It is clear that Year 8 girls are more attracted to the modern option than boys. The graph (see Appendix 2) shows that girls like the idea of having a choice of colours, though both think a sweat shirt is more stylish ...

Factual subheadings help divide up the points. Graphs, charts may be included when relevant, or all attached at the end as numbered appendices.

Conclusion
Sums up what you found out.

Opinions about school uniform
Half of those who responded to our survey were in favour of introducing the modern uniform option, because of its practicality and because it would look smarter than the variety of school dress currently worn ...

You may sum up in short sharp paragraphs, or in numbered points. But the style stays formal.

Recommendations
Some suggestions

Some suggestions
1. Year 8 is in favour of a school uniform.
2. Do not impose a traditional uniform (especially blazers).
3. School sweatshirts in various colours should be introduced.

A list of suggestions completes the report.

Sign and date

Report prepared on behalf of Year 8 Council by:

J Watkins

11 June 1998

summary
- A report is a formal written presentation of information. It is usually organised in the following order: title, terms of reference, findings, conclusions, recommendations.

Questions

A
1. Think of three different kinds of writing all called by the name 'report'. What do they have in common?
2. What do you have to do before you begin to write a report?
3. Look at the notes on the right-hand side of the report extracts. Find three different points describing the style of a report.
4. Which part of a report is intended to influence the actions of your readers?
5. What name is given to extra information attached at the end of a report?

B
1. Make a list of all the reasons mentioned for having a sweatshirt as part of the school uniform.
2. Design a traditional and a modern school uniform for your own school. Write your own report about the advantages and disadvantages of each one. Make sure the writing is divided into sections with subheadings. The style of writing must be formal and impersonal. Include charts, graphs or diagrams (for example, of suggested uniform clothes) within the sections of your report if they help communicate information more clearly. Extra information may be attached to the end, as numbered appendices.

C
Choose another topic relevant to your own school, such as litter, grafitti, road safety, or your local community, for example, places for small children to play or for people your own age to socialise. Carry out some research of your own. Interview people about their opinions, collect statistics, draw maps and diagrams and turn some of your information into graphs and charts. Present your information in a formal report. Make use of visual methods of communication information where they seem most appropriate.

For more information about report writing see pages 64–65 and 80–81

Writing a Letter

> These pages are about how to write different kinds of letter, and how letters compare with other ways of getting in touch with people.

intro

There are many situations in which you will need to be able to write a letter. You must be able to write in a suitable style and lay out your letter correctly.

Formal letters

Formal letters are serious letters to people you do not know very well. Sometimes you may not even know their name, for example if you are writing to a company. They should be written in standard English (see page 2) and be laid out as shown below.

Your address – and phone number if you wish

33 Wood Road
Farnham Hill
HARLEY
Essex
CM13 4LJ
Tel: 01279 0000

Name and address of person you're writing to. If you don't know the name, include a title, such as 'The Manager', or at least a company name

Councillor C. Amrit
The Council House
Broad Street
HARLEY
Essex   CM19 2JD

The date on which you are writing the letter

3 April 1998

Dear Councillor Amrit,

Name of the person you are writing to, or 'Dear Sir/Madam' if you do not know the name

I am replying to your questionnaire about roads in the Farnham Hill area.

Leave a space between paragraphs. Do not indent them unless the letter is handwritten

At present drivers use Farnham Hill as a short-cut during the rush hour. They speed along narrow streets where people live. Two pedestrians have been knocked down recently, and there has been at least one road rage incident.

I think you should install speed bumps and close off Wood Road at the A38 end so that it will not be used in the morning rush hour. I would like to hear your views.

Yours sincerely,

Sonia Lowe

Sonia Lowe

Start 'Yours' with a capital letter. Use 'Yours faithfully' if the letter is very formal and you don't know the name of the person you are writing to

72

Informal letters

An informal letter might be to thank someone, to say sorry, or just to keep in touch with friends and family. You have more freedom in style and layout.

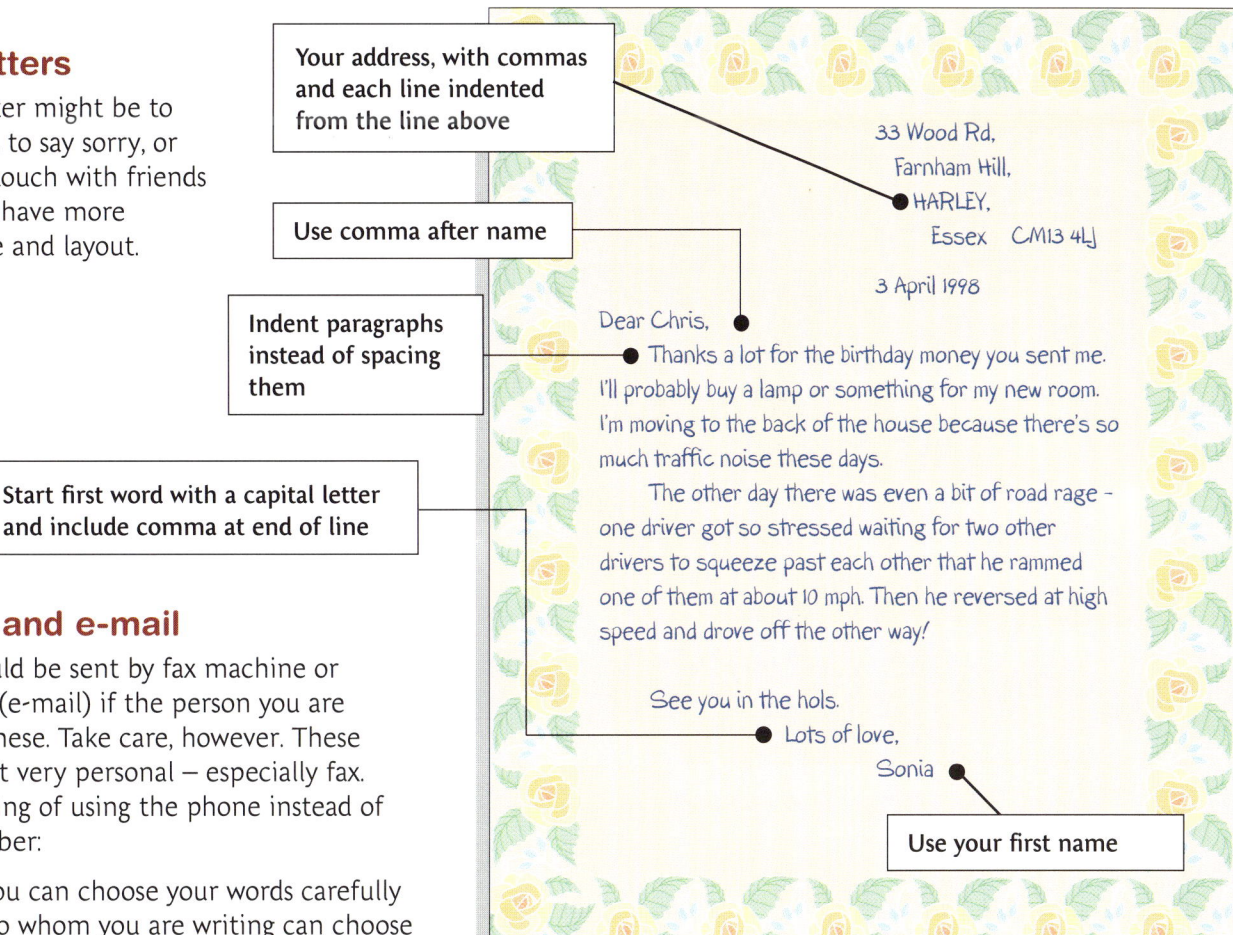

Phone, fax and e-mail

Most letters could be sent by fax machine or electronic mail (e-mail) if the person you are writing to has these. Take care, however. These methods are not very personal – especially fax. If you are thinking of using the phone instead of a letter, remember:

- in a letter, you can choose your words carefully
- the person to whom you are writing can choose when to read it. They can also re-read it to check what you have said.

Your address, with commas and each line indented from the line above

Use comma after name

Indent paragraphs instead of spacing them

Start first word with a capital letter and include comma at end of line

Use your first name

33 Wood Rd,
 Farnham Hill,
  HARLEY,
   Essex CM13 4LJ

3 April 1998

Dear Chris,
 Thanks a lot for the birthday money you sent me. I'll probably buy a lamp or something for my new room. I'm moving to the back of the house because there's so much traffic noise these days.
 The other day there was even a bit of road rage – one driver got so stressed waiting for two other drivers to squeeze past each other that he rammed one of them at about 10 mph. Then he reversed at high speed and drove off the other way!

See you in the hols.
 Lots of love,
  Sonia

---

summary

- Formal letters are for people you do not know well, or do not know at all.
- Formal and informal letters are laid out differently from each other.
- All letters should include your address and begin with 'Dear'. Formal letters should also include the address of the person to whom you are writing.

Questions

A

1. Name two situations in which you would write a formal letter.
2. How should you set out paragraphs in a typed formal letter?
3. Which address can you leave out in an informal letter?
4. Name one way in which a letter is better than phoning.

B

1. Write Councillor Amrit's reply to Sonia's letter.
2. Write an informal letter to a relative.
3. The opening phrase of Sonia's letter to Chris is informal: 'Thanks a lot'. Write down the other informal phrases. Then write more formal phrases to replace each one.

C

Write formally to a councillor about something you would like changed in your area.

73

Letters to the Editor

> These pages are about how to write to newspaper and magazine editors.

intro

Newspapers and magazines often print readers' letters to the editor – the person who decides what gets printed. Most people write because they want to say what they think about an article. Sometimes other people reply to these letters through the editor. Some magazines give prizes for letters.

Letters to an editor should be clearly argued, short and to the point. If you are writing in response to a particular article, say so.

Letter 1

As a Greenshire hunt supporter, I wish to object to your article, '**The truth about fox-hunting**'. — *States position and reason for writing*

Foxes are not 'helpless and harmless'. They kill thousands of chickens every year, carry disease, and spread litter in cities. They need to be controlled, and the best way to do this is by the sport of fox-hunting. — *Argues against the article, giving reasons and conclusions*

I also wish to point out that the article misquotes the Master of the Hunt. He said that opponents of fox-hunting should be 'educated' – not 'taught a lesson'. — *Points out an inaccuracy in the article*

E. Dibley, Greenshire

Note
Set out your letters as on page 72, with your address. Letters here have been simplified by removing addresses.

If you want to write to an editor, follow these rules:

- Read the original article carefully and underline or note down its main points.
- Think about how far you agree or disagree.
- Note what you want to say, and any evidence you have.
- Start by saying why you are writing. End by summing up your views.
- Check that the ideas run on from each other in a way that makes sense. Check that you have not said the same thing twice.

Letters

Letter 2 (a good letter)

You have printed several letters about hunting recently, but none about angling. I am an ex-angler. My reasons for giving it up are as follows.

Although fish are cold-blooded, and not cuddly, they must still suffer. Why else would they try to escape? They cannot cry out in pain, but it cannot be much fun having a hook in your mouth and being pulled from your environment to where you cannot breathe.

Fish do not kill chickens or damage trees. There is no need to control them. Anglers do not even eat the fish they catch. In short, fish deserve to be left in peace.

John Ridley, Sussex

Letter 3 (a bad letter)

Hunting with dogs is cruel. It is not even very efficient. I saw a stag once that was being hunted. It looked terrified. Sometimes it can go on for hours. The stag can die of a heart attack if it's lucky.

It is terrifying for a stag. Eventually they get torn apart by dogs. Fishing is all right. Deer should be shot if they have to be controlled.

I read your article and I just wanted to say this. I am a member of YAH – Youth Against Hunting.

Ruth Palmer

summary

- Letters to an editor should be clearly argued, short and to the point.
- If writing in response to an article, read it carefully, and refer to it in your letter.

Questions

A

1. Give two possible reasons for writing to an editor.
2. Why has the author of Letter 1 written?
3. What three reasons does the author of Letter 1 give for killing foxes?
4. What method does the author of Letter 1 think is best for killing foxes?
5. What do the letters on this page have in common?

B

1. Write a reply to Letter 1 arguing against fox-hunting. Refer to the letter and give your own arguments.
2. Summarise the points made in Letter 2.
3. Write a reply to Letter 2 on behalf of an angling club.
4. Rewrite Letter 3 following the advice above. You can change the words but not the arguments.

C

1. Find a magazine or newspaper with a letters page. Make notes on what each letter is about. Explain how the subjects fit the kind of newspaper or magazine it is.
2. Write a letter to a newspaper or magazine about an article on which you have a strong opinion.

Reading and Comparing Reviews

These pages explain what a review is and how it is written.

intro

A **review** gives a writer's views on a book, exhibition, play or television programme. It helps readers to decide whether to see the play, or watch the programme. Those who have already done so will be interested to compare their experience with the reviewer's.

Look at the storyboard below, for the first episode of a 'soap'.
Then read the reviews. Look out for positive comments, and criticisms.

Reviews

there's hope for soap!

BREDON HILLBILLIES is a brave new youth soap with a difference – it's not Australian and it respects its viewers. Its young actors aren't androids or Barbie dolls, and it is already looking at things that matter to teenagers – like being in a group, and making decisions.

tv review

The first episode's 'Persuasion' theme cleverly linked scenes and introduced main characters. It also showed us settings that we will probably see again, such as the battered but friendly Youth Project and the playground where the kids hang out.

Adults played a background role in the action. This was reinforced by the sensitive photography – big close-ups of teenagers, none of adults.

Most important, right from the opening shot I wanted to know what was going to happen next. And after the tense closing scene of Karen's dad storming into the Project, I'll certainly be switching on for the next episode.

TELEVISION
REVIEW

HILLBILLY BLUES

Episode one of Bredon Hillbillies was a disappointment. The opening shots were promising, but after that the rot set in. Karen's dad, like all the adults, is a cardboard cut-out character. The 'trendy vicar' Rev Trev is almost a joke.

The teenage characters are a little better, helped by some quite good acting – especially from Jasmine Raj as Nina. But they're trapped in a silly, artificial plot that seems determined to show their lives as grim and depressing. I wonder if the writer – Jim Harvey – has ever actually visited a council estate.

Things did look up a bit with the discussion of what the youth project video should be about. This seems to be a clever way to show us teenage lives from behind a camera instead of through one. Perhaps what the teenagers produce will be better than the 'arty' camera work in this episode.

summary

- A review gives a writer's opinions on, for example, some sort of performance.
- Reviews help people decide what to read or watch. They may also want to compare their own experience with the reviewer's.
- The review's language reflects its opinions.

Questions

A

1. Give two reasons why people might read reviews.
2. What theme connects the four scenes of *Bredon Hillbillies*' first episode?
3. What does the first reviewer say is good about the acting?
4. What three positive points does the second review make?

B

1. You are advertising *Bredon Hillbillies*. Find three positive, flattering quotes from the reviews to use – phrases or whole sentences.
2. If you were the writer of *Bredon Hillbillies*, which three phrases or sentences from the reviews would you find most depressing, and why?
3. As the producer of *Bredon Hillbillies*, you want large audiences. Using the reviews, write your advice in a memo to the writer, director and actors.
4. Divide a page into four sections using the following headings: Story, Characters, Acting, Ideas. Write down words and phrases from the reviews that fit each heading. For example, one for 'Acting' might be 'quite good'.

C

Watch an episode of a television 'soap'. Use boxes as in B4 above to make notes. Then review the episode – or review the whole series – focusing on this one episode.

For more information about reviews see pages 78–79

Writing Reviews

A review helps people to decide whether a book, film or CD is worth their time or money.

These pages will help you write book, film and music reviews for different audiences.

When reviewing a book or film you must give readers some idea of the plot (story) and what kind of book or film it is. But remember the following:

- Do not give every little detail. That would be boring.
- Character, style and themes are important too.
- Give your opinions (see pages 82–83).

When writing a review, ask yourself 'How could it have been different?' For example: Were any scenes unnecessary? Should the hero have been more believable? Would you change the ending?

Books and films

If writing about novels, films or plays, try to comment on:

- story
- characters (and, for films and plays, acting)
- style (for a film this mostly means the photography)
- themes (for example love, revenge, learning from mistakes).

Some novels and films — especially films — are of a particular type. Mention the type in your review if appropriate. What types are suggested by the pictures?

Music

It is more difficult to review a piece of music in a way that will make sense to people who have not heard it. However, here are some things to watch out for:

- type of music, for example jungle, hip-hop, dance, indie, house, jazz, classical
- rhythm
- melodies – tunes
- instruments – the way different instruments or sounds work together
- vocals – how a singer sings, compared with other singers
- lyrics – the words.

H

Some adjectives to use in reviews:
exciting dull boring spine-chilling terrifying predictable action-packed unexpected quirky unusual sentimental sad moving tragic hilarious gripping rambling fast-moving energetic repetitive realistic believable bland heart-warming electrifying

A sample review

Here is an example of a film review. Does the film sound like one you'd like to see?

FILMWATCH

Slime (PG)

Karl Bielsperg's new movie, *Slime*, is an all-action thriller about what happens when garden slugs respond unexpectedly to a new kind of pellet. The pellets are meant to finish off our slimey friends for good. Instead, they create a race of super-slugs that munch their way through New York without even pausing to spit out the citizens.

The hero is played by **Tom Hunk**, a gardening expert who persuades the slugs to drown in huge buckets of beer. The love interest comes when he falls for a scientist (**Demi Starlet**) who says that slugs have feelings too, and should be allowed to eat New Jersey for dessert.

The story line is predictable, though entertaining enough if you can believe in super-slugs. The special effects are brilliant, and there are some truly horrific moments helped by close-ups of chomping slug jaws. The acting is convincing, even when the script is not. The love scenes are touching in an old-fashioned way. The main weakness is that the first half of the film – like its concrete-chewing villains – is too slow-moving.

For more information about reviews see pages 76–77

summary

A good review:
- includes description and opinion
- identifies the type of book, film, music, etc., if possible
- comments on story, characters, style and ideas (books, plays and films)
- comments on type, rhythm, melody, instruments, vocals and lyrics (music).

Questions

A

1. Description is one main ingredient of a review. What is the other one?
2. What key question should you ask yourself when writing a review?
3. What four things should you try to comment on in book and film reviews?
4. Where is each of these things mentioned in the review of *Slime*?
5. Place the six things to comment on in music in your own order of importance.

B

1. Use six of the adjectives in the box above in sentences about a book, film or play that you have read or seen. In each case, make it clear what the adjective means.
2. Review a film or television drama. It will help if you make notes soon after watching – or even while watching. It will also help to discuss it with someone else.
3. Review a piece of music or album that you like, explaining why you like it. Make your review suitable for a youth magazine.
4. Review a novel you have read. A useful starting point is the cover 'blurb'.

C

Read the reviews in a magazine or newspaper. Write a review in a style suitable for that magazine or newspaper.

News Reports

These pages are about differences in news reporting between radio, television and newspapers.

A news report must be accurate, interesting and up to the minute. Radio, television and newspapers all have their own advantages:

- Radio has no pictures but news can be phoned in. A reporter with a mobile phone can be on the scene in minutes. Most stations broadcast news every hour.
- Television can film the news – once a camera crew has arrived. Television must have pictures to work well. Most channels have fewer news programmes than on radio.
- Newspapers come out only once a day, but they can combine words with pictures. People can read them at their own speed, and skip or re-read stories.

Compare the radio, television and newspaper reports that follow.

Radio West: 6.00 pm News, 9 September

A major rescue is taking place in Somerset. The leader of a school party has had a heart attack half a mile into a cave, called Swildon's Hole. Two pupils got out and raised the alarm at about 5 o'clock, but three others who set off earlier have not appeared. Rescuers fear they are lost or injured. Reporter Don Macey is at the scene.

Macey: I'm outside a small concrete blockhouse – the unlikely gateway to 10 000 metres of underground passages. Rescuers in wetsuits and helmets are already following a rushing stream into the cave. Some will fan out to search for the missing teenagers. Others will make straight for the cave leader and one remaining boy thought to be with him. The rescuers seem confident, but some say that if the youngsters have taken a wrong turning they could be anywhere.

Police are not naming the teenagers at present. Their head teacher, Brenda Woods, has appealed for calm. She says all six have been caving before and were well equipped.

'Within the last hour three teenagers lost in a Somerset cave have been helped to the surface. Rescuers are still bringing out their teacher …'

'The rescuers are clearly relieved. The three teenagers are emerging from the cave mouth …'

'We kept wandering round and round …'

'I'm delighted that five out of six pupils are now above ground …'

Newspapers

South-West Echo

The best selling local newspaper in the South-West

No. 44,347   10 September

TEENAGE CAVERS SAFE

Six Bristol teenagers have survived an underground ordeal in Swildon's Hole, near Priddy. Their teacher, cave leader David Potts, suffered a heart attack half a mile into the cave, 80 metres below the surface. He is now in Frenchay Hospital.

Two boys and a girl set off for help but became lost in a maze of passages and decided to wait for rescue. Two other pupils, Adam Jones (14) and Lyn Booth (13), waited two hours with the teacher before going for help. They left another boy with the teacher.

The three lost teenagers were brought out at about 9.00 pm, the teacher and remaining boy two hours later.

Police praised the courage of Adam and Lyn, who dived an underwater passage to get back. Lyn commented: 'Mr Potts said to follow the stream all the way. We got very cold and tired, but we're really happy now the others are safe.' (Full story and pictures inside.)

summary

- Radio news relies on sound, but can broadcast quickly.
- Television news must have pictures. It relies less on words.
- Newspapers can use more words, plus pictures.

Questions

A

1. All types of news report have to be accurate. What other things do they have in common?
2. What are the advantages and disadvantages of each?
3. The three news reports show how the rescue story developed. Summarise the new information given in each.
4. Write one-sentence statements for what each group of teenagers (including the boy left behind) did after the teacher fell ill.

B

1. Write a timeline of events for the story, with the times down the left-hand side of the page. Where necessary, work out likely times from those given. Begin with: '1.00 pm: Party enters cave'.
2. Write down the phrases showing Don Macey's efforts to help listeners picture the scene. Suggest three other details he might have included.
3. Write the script of what might have been said in the television report.
4. Write the 'full story' for the newspaper, using your own details. You could add quotations from anyone involved, and suggest pictures.

C

Compare coverage of an event in two different types of report. Hint: record the radio news, or video the television news, then read the newspaper next day. If you cannot record or video the news, make notes. List the ways in which the reports are different.

For more information about reporting news see pages 86–87

Facts and Opinions

These pages are about the difference between facts and opinions, and what a 'factual statement' is.

intro

A **fact** is generally agreed to be true, and can be proven. Here are some examples:

- The first Moonwalk took place in 1969.
- Cows have two stomachs.
- For every 20 men in the world, there are 21 women.

Even if you can't prove a fact yourself, you can usually check it by asking witnesses or looking it up in a reliable book.

An **opinion** is a point of view or belief. For example:

- Pets are a waste of time and money.
- Television is very educational.
- It's time you went to bed.

Factual statements

The adjective (describing word) from fact is **factual**. You can get your facts wrong but still make a **factual statement**. For example: 'Africa is the biggest country in the world'. (Wrong: it's not a country.) This is not an opinion. Can you think of another incorrect factual statement?

People don't always agree on what the facts are. We must then weigh up the evidence and the reliability of the information. Some words we might use are: perhaps; might; it is possible that; probably; almost certainly. **Perhaps** you'll be able to think of sentences using all of these. You'll **probably** think of a few. You'll **almost certainly** manage one!

The news item below contains facts and opinions.

H

Don't be fooled by how an opinion is presented:

- The **fact** is, they're all too lazy. (Calling something a fact doesn't make it one.)
- It's **common knowledge** that we need more teachers. (This suggests that if you don't agree, you're ignorant of something everyone else knows.)
- World population **will** double by 2010. (The use of 'will', and the figures, makes it sound like a scientifically proven fact.)

SCHOOL PARTY'S HOLD-UP HORROR

Two masked men yesterday held up a party of schoolchildren on a trip to the Natural History Museum. Brushing aside the plucky resistance of teacher Valerie Pugh, the hard-hearted pair demanded the children's packed lunches and sweets. The only good thing about this shocking and cowardly crime is that sweets are probably the worst thing you can eat anyway.

Newspapers

summary

- A fact is generally agreed to be true, and can be proven.
- An opinion is a point of view or belief.
- A factual statement is not necessarily correct.
- If the facts are not certain, we use words such as 'perhaps' and 'might'.

Questions

A

1. Divide the following statements into facts and opinions:
   a) United deserve to win.
   b) Fleas can jump many times their own height.
   c) Children grow up faster these days.
   d) Donna is taller than Kevin.
   e) The Queen is the richest woman in Britain.
   f) Eating people is wrong.
2. Write down the words or phrases containing opinions in the news item opposite.

B

1. Look at the burglary story. Write down two facts and two opinions about each of the pictures.
2. Record the facts of the case shown in the pictures and speech bubbles.
3. Write a news feature about the crime, making it clear what is fact and what is only probable. Quote at least one opinion.

C

Write a paragraph about your area. Include at least three facts and three opinions.

Young, unemployed, under 5'6", probably hungry, an amateur... They've no sense of right and wrong, these kids...

It's a shame – he's a nice old man... It takes me ten minutes from school and we finish at 3.20. I saw this man, right? He was running down the street really fast. He must have been scared. He had a grey-hooded sweatshirt and blue tracksuit bottoms.

It was 4 o'clock. I'd only just got in – the bus service here is terrible. I heard a noise. I said, 'Who's that?' I went into the kitchen, and the fridge was open, and there was the little blighter escaping out the window. He had a blue anorak and jeans on. Couldn't see his face. They ought to lock 'em up and throw away the key. This used to be a nice estate.

Bias

These pages explain bias, and the ways in which news reports can be biased.

When a referee ignores fouls by a team he or she likes and penalises the other team, he or she is **biased**. The referee is judging unfairly because he or she likes one team more than the other.

When news reporters allow their own views to affect the way they write about the news, this is also bias. Bias does not mean actually lying about the facts – just presenting them in an unbalanced way. This can be done deliberately or unintentionally.

> If a report is **unbiased** and gives a fair, balanced view of all the facts, we can say it is **objective**. The opposite of bias is **objectivity**.

There are three main types of bias:

- emotive language
- selection – leaving things out
- exaggeration and underplaying.

Emotive language

This means using words that affect the reader's emotions. For example:

A A gang of youths was hanging around outside the shop staring at people and muttering.

B A group of young men was waiting outside the shop watching passers-by and chatting quietly.

The facts are the same in A and B. Pick out the words that make the 'youths' in version A seem threatening.

Selection

This means deliberately including some facts while leaving out others. In the following example, what difference would it make if the words in bold were left out?

*The school has never had an exam failure **because none of its pupils has ever taken any exams**. It has a well-equipped computing centre **but no classrooms**.*

Exaggeration and underplaying

Exaggeration is best explained by an example:

The Liverpool striker found a gap the size of a battleship in Sheffield's defence and torpedoed the ball into the net. The Sheffield goalie looked as if he was about to start blubbering like a 2-year-old.

Underplaying is the opposite of exaggeration. It means making something smaller or less important than it really is. Here is an example:

The arrest of the Prime Minister's son for trying to burn down Buckingham Palace has been a slight, temporary setback for the government. A government spokesman blamed 'youthful high spirits', and added, 'This sort of thing happens all the time in politics.'

Which caption?

Which caption do you think fits the picture opposite?

- Lunchtime drinking leads to President's downfall
- The President demonstrates his gymnastic ability
- The President loses his grip
- A crazed rock music fan pulls the President from his helicopter
- The President 'monkeys about' for reporters.

Newspapers

summary

- A biased report is one which is one-sided or unfair in the way it presents facts.
- Bias can be deliberate or unintentional.
- There are three main types of bias: emotive language, selection and exaggeration.

Questions

A

1. Write down in your own words what bias is.
2. 'The new road will gouge a wound in the countryside.' What kind of bias is this?
3. 'The prime minister has the brain of a budgie.' What kind of bias is this?
4. What kind of bias plays on the reader's emotions?

B

1. Copy the biased words in this news report of Harold's defeat in 1066. Explain how they are biased:

   'The Battle of Hastings, fought yesterday by brave King Harold and William, the nasty little Norman, came close to being Harold's greatest victory. Harold's heroes had marched proudly from the north, where they had been busy thrashing the Vikings. William and his gang of cut-throats plucked up courage to sneak ashore only when Harold's back was turned. Harold swatted the Norman nitwits like flies. People are already calling him Harold the Great. He is expected to recover from his eye injury soon.'

2. Write an unbiased account of the Battle of Hastings from the facts above.
3. Write a biased description of your room. Make it sound wonderful without lying.
4. Headlines can be biased. Write biased opening paragraphs to follow these headlines about people protesting against a new road being built:

   Hairy hippies block path of progress

   Protesters' heroic fight to save countryside

C

Find a newspaper report that you think is biased. Remember that headlines and captions can be biased as well as the main text. Get permission to cut it out. Mark on it what you think is biased. Explain why you have marked what you have.

For more information about emotive language see pages 92–93

Writing a News Feature

> These pages are about how to write news reports and editorials.

intro

News features must be easy to follow. They must also start with the most important information and give the less important details later. This is for two reasons:

- Readers want to get the key facts quickly. They will only read to the end if the story interests them.
- A newspaper has limited space. If the important information comes at the beginning of a feature, the end can be cut if necessary.

The journalist's triangle

The triangle below shows an example of how to arrange information in a news feature, with the most important information coming first.

What, who, where, when, why? — *There was confusion in Alton High Street yesterday when a lorry crashed into the open-air market. Driver Dan Plum (33) had swerved to avoid a schoolboy cyclist.*

How? Further details — *The lorry hit a fruit stall run by Mrs Nina Kumari. Apples and oranges were scattered for 50 metres down the road. Luckily no one was hurt.*

Extras, quotes. — *The schoolboy, Jason Barter (13), helped passers-by to pick up the fruit. He said his mind had been on his homework. A police spokesperson said: 'This could have been a very nasty accident. Luckily it was more of a fruit salad.'*

Editorials

Newspapers often have an **editorial** section in which a journalist comments on recent news. This contains opinions as well as facts (see pages 82–83). Read the editorial comment, and the notes to see how it works.

EDITORIAL COMMENT

States the newspaper's position and past record — The *Alton Gazette* always encourages schemes offering challenge and adventure to youngsters. Its 'Young Journalist of the Year' award produced some excellent young reporters.

Gives reason for the editorial — That is why we feel we have a right to comment on the growing popularity of girls' boxing in the town.

Lists possible arguments for girls' boxing, ending with a rhetorical question (one asked for effect, without expecting an answer). — Of course girls should have the same rights as boys. Of course girls need challenges and have a part to play in the world of sport. But does this justify girls as young as 11 throwing punches at each other to entertain a howling crowd?

Concludes with an appeal — Let girls go canoeing, climbing, sailing if they must. But please, let's end this unfeminine brutality before a girl gets badly hurt.

Newspapers

H

Clichés are phrases that are used too often. Bad or overworked journalists sometimes use them.
Here are some to avoid:
- a level playing field (a fair situation)
- at the end of the day (as in 'At the end of the day, it's just a game')
- got under way (began)
- ground to a halt (stopped)
- at this moment in time (now)
- a dramatic development (an unexpected turn of events)

summary

- News features must be easy to follow and give the important information first.
- Use the 'journalist's triangle' to arrange your information.
- An editorial gives opinions about recent news.

Questions

A

1. Why should important information go at the start of a news feature, not at the end?
2. What five questions will give you the important details of a news event?
3. Where should a quotation from a witness or spokesperson normally go — at the beginning or the end?
4. What does the *Alton Gazette* reporter think about girls' boxing?

B

1. Neatly draw five boxes, labelled What? Who? Where? When? Why? Use them to record the key facts of the events shown (in the wrong order) in these five pictures. Then write the news story.
2. Use the 'five boxes' to record the details of something important that has happened to you recently, or of a local event.

C

1. Write an editorial similar to the one on these pages. Use it to give your own views on girls' boxing or on recent news.
2. Find a front-page news story that interests you, or make notes on a television news story. Write down the key facts. Add two questions a reporter might want answered in order to write a more detailed and interesting story.

For more information about news reports see pages 80–81

87

Understanding Adverts

intro

Advertisements have to grab our attention. Some of the ways they do this are shown below.

These pages are about advertisements and how they get people to spend money on the things that they are advertising.

Romance

ATTENTION

The ridiculous

Celebrity

Memories are made of this

The longer an advertisement holds our attention, the more we will remember it. If we remember it, we're well on the way to buying the product or service. Remember, in advertising: **being remembered matters more than being believed**.

Most of the things that grab attention also help us remember. For example:

- anything that tells a story — this is easiest on television, but even a billboard poster can do this (see the Nissan poster)
- anything funny, especially if we have to wait for the punchline — puns (double meanings) and word-plays work well (see the poster)
- slogans — catchy, clever-sounding phrases that are fun to say
- jingles — slogans set to music.

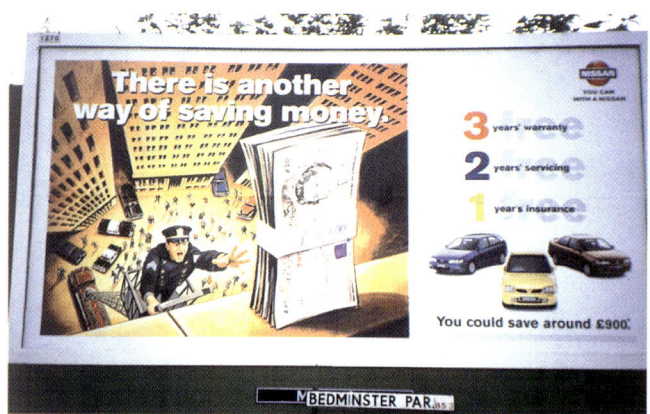

88

Leaflets and Adverts

You know it's true!

Advertisements may also try to persuade. Some ways they do this are:

- by using scientific 'evidence' including an expert's word
- by telling you what's good about the product
- by suggesting that it will make you happier, safer or more popular.

F

Companies advertise wherever they can get attention, on buses and trains, hot air balloons, the Internet – even school exercise books. The main places are:

- television
  (including televised sports events such as motor racing)
- magazines and newspapers
- billboards
- radio (mostly local businesses).

WE, THE UNDERSIGNED PLEDGE ALLEGIANCE TO FELIX.

JOIN FELIX'S GANG. 3 MILLION STRONG AND GROWING.

summary

- Advertisements have to get your attention and stay in your memory.
- Some try to persuade you, for example by telling you that the product will make you happier or healthier.

Questions

A

1. Name three advertising techniques for getting attention.
2. What pun is used by Nissan in its advertisement?
3. What is offered 'free' in the Nissan advertisement?
4. How does the Felix advertisement make cats seem human?

B

1. Explain the double meaning in the Nissan advertisement, and what 'story' the main picture shows.
2. Explain how the Felix advertisement will get people to buy Felix cat food.
3. Think of a product. Describe a deliberately ridiculous image to advertise it.
4. From memory, write short descriptions of four advertisements. Explain what you think has made you remember each one.

C

1. As you watch a television commercial break, note down what each advertisement is for. Then make a table to show
   (a) the name of each product or service and what it is;
   (b) what happens in the advertisement;
   (c) how the advertisement gets attention; and
   (d) what helps you to remember it.
2. Find a magazine or newspaper advertisement that uses words and a picture to persuade you to buy something. Write a paragraph about how it tries to do this. Think about how the words work with the picture.

For more information about adverts see pages 90–91

Writing Adverts

intro

When a company hires an advertising agency to write an advert for a product, the agency will want to know about:

- the selling points of the product or service (special features)
- who the product or service is aimed at.

These pages are about how to combine words with pictures to create advertisements that appeal to a particular audience.

Sometimes it is easy to identify selling points. For example:

> Passenger air bags, side-window de-misters and a unique anti-spin steering system – all for under £10,000 on the road!

If the product has no unique selling points, advertisers have to focus on **image**:

> Eureka – a deodorant for people who live in the fast lane
>
> Café soir – the coffee with style

The image will be designed to appeal to the **target audience** – the people who will see (or hear) and respond to the advertisement. For example:

- teenagers who like to think that they're rebels
- middle-aged people worried about money
- older people able to afford luxuries.

Look at the advertisements on these pages. Think about:

- who they are aimed at
- the product image
- how the words and pictures work together.

[Comic strip:]

- "The gold – it's gone! Brown, seal all exits!"
- "That smell ..."
- "Too late, she'll be long gone."
- "What made you follow me?"
- "It was the Gold."
- "Gold fragrance. Get the Gold, get the guy."

90

Leaflets and Adverts

Get a Taste of Adventure with Mars®
Buy a Mars® Bar and you could instantly WIN TRAILFINDERS travel worth up to £1200 to anywhere in the world
Plus EVERY promotional bar is worth £1* OFF selected ROUGH GUIDES

Mars — THE TASTE OF ADVENTURE
*up to a maximum of £3-£5 per guide, depending on title.

Summary

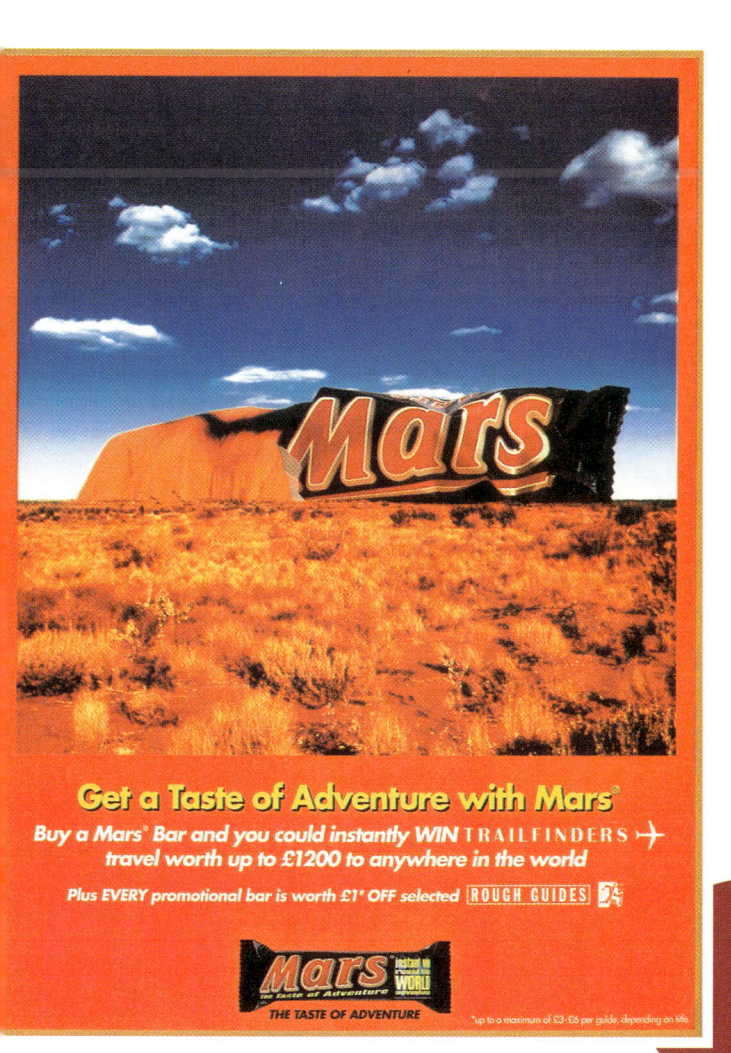

- Identify the product's selling points and image, and who is meant to buy it.
- In most advertisements, words and pictures must work together.

Questions

A

1. What two things must an advertising agency know about a product?
2. What is meant by 'target audience'?
3. Think of a product in your home that has selling points. Name three that could be used to advertise it.
4. Think of a product in your home that has a particular image. Say what the image is and what sort of person would be attracted by it.
5. Name products that would appeal to the target audiences listed above – one product for each audience.

B

1. Think about something you have bought, and why you bought it. List six reasons why someone should buy the product. Example: 'It's completely waterproof.'
2. Describe in words, or draw, a storyboard like the one above for a television advertisement for a product you like.
3. Make up a magazine advertisement for a product in your home, using words with pictures. The words could describe the product's selling points, or its image.

C

Make up an advertisement for a product or service advertised on television or in a magazine. Your advertisement must be part of the same advertising campaign. For example, if the original advertisement uses a story, yours could continue it.

For more information about adverts see pages 88–89

Charity Appeals

intro

Charities raise money to help the starving, the homeless and the sick. Animal charities raise money to protect animals threatened with extinction or cruelty. To get this money, they have to make appeals.

These pages are about the kind of language and pictures used in charity appeals.

Unlike ordinary advertisements, charity appeals have to make us give without getting a product in return. They use facts and figures to show how bad a problem is, but they also need to stir our **feelings** – especially our sympathy. They often do this through language that makes us imagine the suffering of other people, or animals. This is called **emotive language**.

▶ *This UNICEF appeal was in a national newspaper. It gives facts and figures, and uses some emotive language.*

decimated	=	almost completely destroyed
vulnerable to	=	easily hurt by
deteriorates	=	gets worse

SOMALIA FLOOD EMERGENCY
43 villages washed away and more rain forecast

In the worst floods to hit Somalia in over 30 years, the Jubba and Shabbeleh valleys are under water. Hundreds of people have already drowned and over 15,000 houses have been destroyed. By the time you've read this appeal, more homes will have been washed away.

150,000 people have been forced to flee their homes and are now facing appalling conditions - living in trees or huddling together on islets of dry land. With contaminated water, cholera and malaria epidemics are a real threat.

The most at risk are the children. The water is infested with deadly snakes and crocodiles. Crops and stores of food have been decimated - a malnourished child is especially vulnerable to disease.

UNICEF (the United Nations Children's Fund) is leading the humanitarian relief operation. We urgently need your help to provide waterproof sheeting for emergency shelter, medicines to prevent the spread of diseases, blankets and special food for the smallest children. **It costs just £5 to buy and transport enough high-energy food to sustain one child for a month.**

As each hour goes by, the situation deteriorates. Heavy rain and worse floods are expected over the next few days. The only way to reach the children is by air and by boat.

Please, if you can, send a donation to UNICEF *today* - and help us keep the children of Somalia alive.

UNICEF EMERGENCY CHILDREN'S APPEAL
0345 312 312
24HR LOCAL RATE CREDIT CARD DONATION LINE

Here is my gift of: ☐ £25 ☐ £50 ☐ £75 ☐ £100 I prefer to give £ _____
(Please make your cheque/postal order payable to UNICEF)

A gift of £250 or more qualifies for Gift Aid. This means it is worth almost a third extra to UNICEF as the Inland Revenue will refund to us the tax you have already paid on your gift.

OR, Please debit my Switch/Delta/MasterCard/Visa/Amex/Diners Club/CAF card
(Please delete as appropriate)

Switch Issue _____ Expiry Date _____ Signature _____
Name _____ Address _____
_____ Postcode _____

Please post this coupon with your gift to UNICEF, Room GUA1, FREEPOST, Chelmsford CM2 8BR.
We occasionally allow like-minded charities to write to our supporters. To be excluded tick here ☐
Registered Charity No. 207595

unicef
United Nations Children's Fund

Leaflets and Adverts

> This animal charity billboard poster gets its message across to passing drivers.

summary

- A charity appeal tries to persuade people to give money.
- It may use emotive language to do this: language that gets to our emotions.
- Charity appeals normally use words and pictures together.

Questions

A

1. What do the words *prisoner-of-war* and *thug* make you feel? How are they used to win sympathy in the Blue Cross appeal?
2. The cross in 'Joe + Trixi' has two meanings. What are they?
3. What sentence in the first paragraph of the Somalia appeal helps us to realise how urgent the situation is?
4. Name two ways in which a Somalian child might die due to the flood.
5. What exactly is the Somalian appeal asking readers to do?

B

1. Choose words to complete the Blue Cross 'equation': Joe + Trixi = ?
2. Write a paragraph explaining the full message contained in the Blue Cross appeal.
3. Why do you think charity appeals like the Blue Cross one use an individual with a name? Write new words for the Somalia appeal naming the children in the picture and describing their experiences in the flood.
4. The phrase *huddling together* in the Somalia appeal (paragraph 2) is an example of emotive language. Rewrite the first three paragraphs using more emotive language to make readers imagine the suffering of the Somalian children.

C

Find a charity appeal leaflet or advertisement. Read it carefully. Mark or note persuasive language, facts or figures. Write a paragraph explaining how they work.

For more information about emotive language see pages 84–85

Warnings and Advice

intro

Charities, pressure groups and the government all produce materials aimed to warn people or change how they behave. Why? Here are some examples:

- The Royal Society for the Protection of Animals (RSPCA, a charity) tries to get people to treat animals better.
- Greenpeace (a pressure group) wants to stop pollution and save animal species.
- The government wants people to live healthy lifestyles so that they won't place a strain on family doctors and hospitals.

These pages are about understanding and producing posters, advertisements and leaflets designed to change how people behave.

Any attempt to change how people behave must first look at why they behave as they do. It will include **facts**, and sometimes **opinions** and **arguments**. It will offer alternatives. (For more on facts, opinions and arguments, see pages 74–75 and 82–83.)

Posters

These must be eye-catching. The image is very important. It should work with the words and help to carry the message. The RSPCA poster would not be so effective if it just used a photograph of a dog. Why?

Advertisements

These must be eye-catching too, but they can use more words, because the reader will probably be sitting down, relaxing and feel more like reading. If they are in a magazine, their style must appeal to the kind of people who read the magazine.

94

Leaflets and Adverts

Leaflets

A leaflet folds into pages. The front page must be eye-catching and not have too much writing on it. The next page normally gives more information, followed by the arguments, then the appeal for action. Look at this page from an anti-smoking leaflet.

TICK TOCK IT'S TIME TO STOP!

STOPPING

Stopping smoking for good is a big step, so remember:

- Take it one day at a time.
- Make your goal getting through today.
- Don't worry about tomorrow.
- Each day congratulate yourself on having made it so far.

Summary

- Charities, pressure groups and the government publish materials to change behaviour. These contain facts, opinions, arguments and alternatives. They can be in the form of posters, advertisements or leaflets. They must be eye-catching.
- Posters must use few words. Leaflets can use the most.

Questions

A

1. Which of the following things do persuasive materials always include: opinions, arguments, facts, alternatives?
2. Which use more words — posters or leaflets?
3. What is eye-catching about the materials on these pages?

B

1. Explain how the picture in the RSPCA advertisement works with the words to persuade people to be responsible about pets.
2. Describe the picture from the anti-smoking leaflet and explain its message.
3. Design a magazine advertisement either
   (a) to stop young people smoking, or
   (b) to make drivers slow down.
   Possible techniques: cartoon strip, bullet points, case study, scientific evidence.

C

Think of a behaviour change that would improve your area. Design a leaflet arguing your case. Give it an eye-catching cover, include facts (make up statistics if necessary), arguments and a plan of action. Suggestions: crime, litter, cars, dogs, friendliness.

Diaries and Letters

These pages are about expressing personal views in diaries and letters.

Diaries and letters are probably the most popular forms of writing. Most people at some time or another have kept a diary. It is important to have the chance to express your personal feelings, and a diary is a private place where you can think about them. Writing your thoughts down often makes them clearer.

Choosing a style

Letters give you the opportunity to communicate your personal feelings and ideas to a particular person or, if you are writing to a newspaper, to a wide audience.

Because diaries and letters are so personal there is a great deal of freedom in styles of writing. They can contain:

- jokes
- slang
- codes and made-up words
- drawings and cartoons.

However, like all good writing they should be written in an interesting and imaginative way. Some personal diaries and collections of letters which were not written to be seen by anyone else have become international bestsellers because they are so lively and informative.

Diary writing

An example of a fictional diary which is lively and humorous is *The Secret Diary of Adrian Mole Aged 13¾* by the modern writer Sue Townsend. This is the first entry:

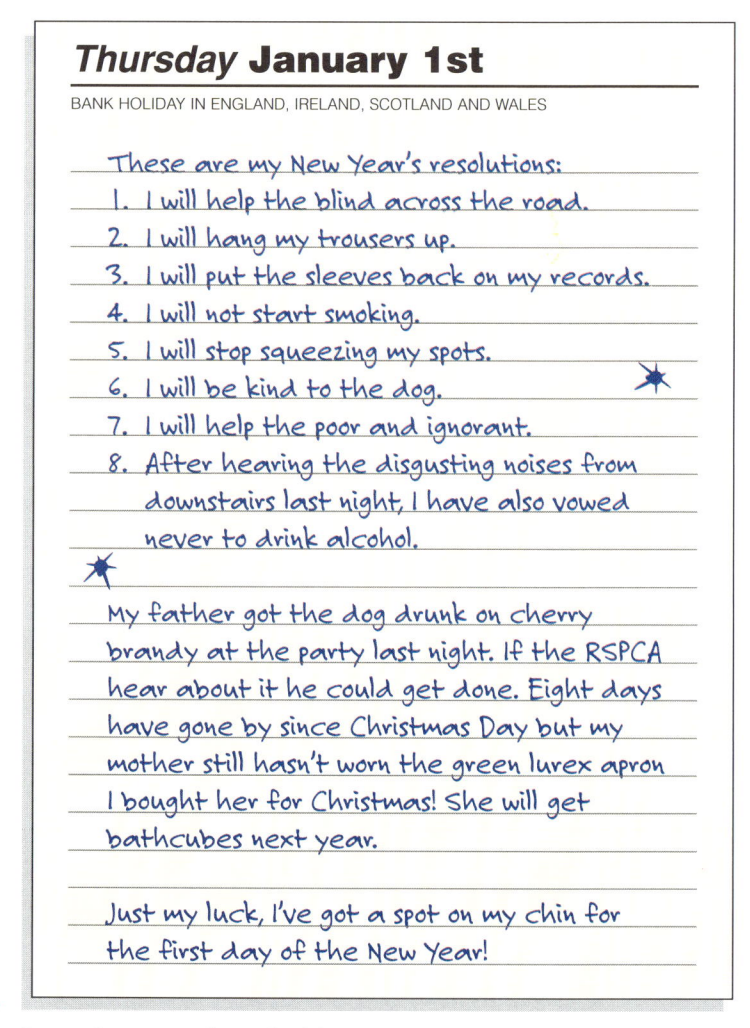

> **Thursday January 1st**
> BANK HOLIDAY IN ENGLAND, IRELAND, SCOTLAND AND WALES
>
> These are my New Year's resolutions:
> 1. I will help the blind across the road.
> 2. I will hang my trousers up.
> 3. I will put the sleeves back on my records.
> 4. I will not start smoking.
> 5. I will stop squeezing my spots.
> 6. I will be kind to the dog.
> 7. I will help the poor and ignorant.
> 8. After hearing the disgusting noises from downstairs last night, I have also vowed never to drink alcohol.
>
> My father got the dog drunk on cherry brandy at the party last night. If the RSPCA hear about it he could get done. Eight days have gone by since Christmas Day but my mother still hasn't worn the green lurex apron I bought her for Christmas! She will get bathcubes next year.
>
> Just my luck, I've got a spot on my chin for the first day of the New Year!

from *The Secret Diary of Adrian Mole aged 13¾* by Sue Townsend

Notice how the writer picks out just certain details to make the diary entertaining.

Literary Non-fiction

Letter writing

When writing letters it is also necessary to select the information that is most important. In the following two extracts from letters by the twentieth-century Irish dramatist George Bernard Shaw he writes very clearly and directly. The first extract is from a letter to a friend whose son has just been killed in the First World War.

Never saw it or heard about it until your letter came. It is no use: I can't be sympathetic: these things simply make me furious. I want to swear. I do swear. Killed just because people are blasted fools ...

Oh damn, damn, damn, damn, damn, damn, damn, damn, damn, damn, damn, DAMN, DAMN!

And oh, dear, dear, dear, dear, dear, dear, dearest!

G.B.S.

from *Collected Letters of George Bernard Shaw* by George Bernard Shaw

The second letter contains very different feelings. He wrote it on the day that his wife died.

Charlotte died this morning at 2.30. You saw what she had become when you last visited us: an old woman bowed and crippled, furrowed and wrinkled, and greatly distressed by hallucinations of crowds in the room, evil persons and animals ...

But on Friday evening a miracle began. Her troubles vanished. Her visions ceased. Her furrows and wrinkles smoothed out. Forty years fell off her like a garment. She had thirty hours of happiness and heaven. Even after her last breath she shed another twenty years, and now lies young and incredibly beautiful ... I did not know I could be so moved.

Notice how the writer is not trying to write an essay, he is just expressing his feelings in a very personal way.

summary
- Diaries and letters give you the opportunity to express your personal feelings and thoughts.
- You can choose whichever style of writing you prefer.
- It is important to select information carefully.

Questions

A
1. Why do people write diaries and letters?
2. What are four different ways that a writer might 'liven up' a diary or letter?
3. Why do you need to select the information you want to include in a diary or letter carefully?

B
1. In *The Secret Diary of Adrian Mole* how has the writer made the diary interesting?
2. What do we learn about the character of the person writing this diary?
3. In the second letter about the death of George Bernard Shaw's wife what are the different emotions expressed?
4. In this letter Shaw uses some very effective description. Find an example of a word or phrase that you like and say why you chose it.

C
Write a series of diary entries over the next week picking out just a few memorable details from each day. These could be feelings or thoughts or dreams you have, interesting things you do or people you meet.

Biography and Autobiography

intro

A **biography** is the story of a person's life written by someone who either knows that person well or who has studied the details of his or her life. Many people like to read biographies of famous actors, sports personalities, pop stars or public figures.

An **autobiography** is a written account of one's own life and therefore normally written in the first person.

These pages are about biographical and autobiographical writing.

Getting to know the person

The important thing to remember about biographies and autobiographies is that they are a kind of story. Writers use the same techniques that they use in story writing to make the biography or autobiography interesting to the reader.

The purpose of the biographer or autobiographer is to help the reader really get to know the person he or she is writing about and to find out some of the details of the person's life. One of the hardest decisions is to work out which details to include and which to leave out. This is why a famous person might have several biographies written about him or her — each biographer will choose to describe different details about the individual's life according to what the writer wishes to say about the person.

If you were to write your own autobiography, which parts of your life would you want to describe and which would you leave out? Why would you make these choices?

Autobiography

A well-known autobiography was written by the twentieth-century author Laurie Lee. He called the first part *Cider with Rosie*, and describes growing up in a small village in the South West of England. He starts the book at the age of 3 and writes from the point of view of himself as a young child.

I was set down from the carrier's cart at the age of three; and there with a sense of bewilderment and terror my life in the village began.

The June grass, amongst which I stood, was taller than I was, and I wept. I had never been so close to grass before. It towered above me and all around me, each blade tatooed with tiger-skins of sunlight.

Literary Non-fiction

It was knife-edged, dark, and a wicked green, thick as a forest and alive with grasshoppers that chirped and chattered and leapt through the air like monkeys.

I was lost and didn't know where to move. A tropic heat oozed up from the ground, rank with sharp odours of roots and nettles. Snow-clouds of elder-blossom banked in the sky, showering upon me the fumes and flakes of their sweet and giddy suffocation. High overhead ran frenzied larks, screaming, as though the sky were tearing apart.

For the first time in my life I was out of the sight of humans. For the first time in my life I was alone in a world whose behaviour I could neither predict nor fathom: a world of birds that squealed, of plants that stank, of insects that sprang about without warning. I was lost and I did not expect to be found again. I put back my head and howled, and the sun bit me smartly on the face, like a bully.

from **Cider with Rosie** by Laurie Lee

Notice how Laurie Lee paints a very clear picture of the setting and puts the reader into the mind of the young boy. Notice also how the writer has chosen unusual and highly imaginative, descriptive words to catch the reader's attention.

Biography

Many biographies start in the same colourful way, giving the readers a picture of a scene to help them get involved with the story. The biography of Steven Spielberg, the film director, written by Andrew Yule, starts off with a dramatic scene from Spielberg's childhood.

It grew overnight into a palpable thing, a live entity with darkly mocking features ... It grew and grew until he was unable to see over, under or past it, until its poisonous shadow threatened to obliterate the rest of his life ... The grey light of dawn, when at last it came, only served to confirm that today was the day – the day he'd been dreading for weeks, the day when he, Steven Spielberg, together with the rest of his elementary class of fifty pupils, was due to run a mile to gain a grade.

The awful reality outdid even his worst imaginings. The remainder of the class had crossed the finishing line, leaving just two trailing behind. One – a skinny, spindly legged boy, tall for his age, large head precariously balanced on a pipe-stem neck – was

a hundred yards short; the other, forty yards behind ..., his chubby features red and running with sweat, his legs wobbling and chaffing as they rubbed together.

Suddenly the entire class was rooting for the straggler, shouting, 'C'mon, c'mon, beat Spielberg! You can do it! Beat the wimp! You can do it! Run, run!'

from **Steven Spielberg, Father to the Man** by Andrew Yule

The purpose of the writer is to create interest and make us want to read on just as if he were writing a fictional story.

Summary
- Biographies and autobiographies tell the story of someone's life.
- The writer must decide which details to include in the story to give a clear and interesting picture of the person concerned.

Questions

A

1. What type of story is a biography?
2. How does an autobiography differ from a biography?
3. Would you expect an autobiography to be written in the first or the third person?
4. Is Laurie Lee's book, *Cider with Rosie*, an autobiography or a biography?

B

1. Pick out three lines or phrases from the opening to *Cider with Rosie* that tell us the story is written through the eyes of a 3-year-old child.
2. What picture does Laurie Lee want to paint of the young boy and his surroundings?
3. Pick out three examples of words and phrases from this extract that you think are effective. For each one say why you chose it and what is interesting about the language.
4. In the biography of Steven Spielberg what is the first impression we get of the young Spielberg? Pick out examples from the text to back up your answer.

C

Write a mini-biography of someone you know well or are very interested in. Find out as many details as you can about the person's life and organise the information carefully. Remember to make the writing as colourful and lively as possible.

For more information on writing in the first and third person narrative see pages 116–117

Travel Writing

> These pages are about how writers approach the subject of travel and how to write effectively about it.

intro

One of the exciting things about travelling is having new and unusual experiences. If we go to a part of the country we have not been to before, we will see different landscapes and scenery, visit new buildings, hear different accents and taste local food. If we go to a foreign country, everything will be even more unusual including: language, manners and customs, clothes, food and eating times, and climate.

Writing about places

Many people write about their travels. It can be a permanent record of their experiences rather like taking photographs but with more details. It can also be a way of sharing their experiences with people who do not know about these places.

Whatever the reason for travel writing it is very important to create a vivid picture of the place so that anyone reading it will be able to imagine what it is like there. It is also important to write about your impressions of the place so the reader can 'feel' the atmosphere.

Strange experiences

Bruce Chatwin is a twentieth-century travel writer who visited many parts of the world, writing about the people he met and the thoughts and feelings he had while travelling. In this extract he is travelling in Nepal, near Mount Everest in the Himalayas. He is searching for evidence of the Yeti or Abominable Snowman, a legendary ape-like creature said to live on the mountain slopes. Suddenly he sees some tracks.

H

> If you want to write about places you visit, it is important to keep a diary so you can record detailed descriptions as well as names and unusual phrases that people might use. Notice how many details and specific names there are in the extracts.

'Look!' I blurted out. 'Yeti tracks!'
'Oh yeah?' drawled Elizabeth, and went on watching shelldrake.
'Look at them!'
On the north-facing slope behind us there was a line of very strange footprints. They were each about fifteen inches long, wider at the top than the heel, and on some you saw – or thought you saw – the imprint of a giant big toe.
They approached the base of an almost vertical bank, stopped, continued on the slope higher up, and finally petered out along a rocky ridge. I reckoned that the creature had jumped at least eight feet into the air and twelve along. The tracks were perhaps a day old and had melted a little; even so I could see that they hadn't been made by any of the usual contenders – yak, blue bear, snow leopard, langur monkey, human or human hoaxer. No hoaxer could have jumped that high, yet the Sherpas say that Yeti habitually jumps his own height and more ...
I was sure there must be some logical explanation and called Sangye over.
'Did you ever,' I asked, 'on any of your treks, see anything like them?'
'Never,' he said, darkly. 'they were not made by men.'
'Then who made them?'
'Same as Yeti.'

100

Literary Non-fiction

> **summary**
>
> - Good travel writing will give the reader a 'feel' for the place that is being described. The writer needs to pick out those details which will capture the atmosphere of the place as well as the writer's own thoughts and feelings.

Later on Chatwin describes the scene around them where they camped and then the next stage of the journey.

> We camped at Gokyo and in the afternoon I climbed the summit of Gokyo Ri where, gasping for oxygen at 18,000 feet, I propped myself against a stone cairn and, while the wind ripped at the prayer flags, gazed dully at the ring of blue and white peaks – Cho Oyu, Everest, Lhotse, Nuptse and, far to the east, the cone of Makalu.
> The sky was all but cloudless; a stream of grey vapour crept up the valley from India, and above it, in the opposite direction, a few shreds of cumulus came blowing out of Tibet …
> At sundown it started to freeze. I had a headache and could only sleep fitfully. All night I heard, or imagined, strange rumbles and half-expected a hairy hand to rip through the roof of the tent …
> After Gokyo the weather turned sour. Clouds hung below the snowline and snowflakes whizzed in our faces. We stopped at a tea house called 'Cho Oyu view' where the boy called out 'Milik tea or balak tea?' and gave us boiled potatoes and hot chillie peppers. We got stuck behind a caravan of fourteen yaks nose to tail which Elizabeth said looked like a 'hairy black centipede'. Across the main valley we saw the monastery of Thyangboche and heard the weird music of horns and cymbals carried on the morning wind.

from ***What am I doing here?*** by Bruce Chatwin

Questions

A

1. If you visit a foreign country and wish to write about your experiences, why is it a good idea to keep a diary?
2. Why are people interested in reading travel books?
3. In the first extract by Bruce Chatwin what makes him think the tracks were made by a Yeti?
4. In the second extract what details tell us that we are in a different country from our own?

B

1. How do you think Bruce Chatwin felt when he saw the Yeti tracks? Find some evidence from the extract to back up your answer.
2. How does this compare with the way he felt that night in his tent?
3. What picture do you get of the place that Bruce Chatwin describes? Write a paragraph describing the area in your own words.
4. Write a page for a holiday brochure attracting holiday-makers to this area. How would you make it sound exciting and attractive?

C

1. Write your own piece of travel description based on a short visit or a longer trip you have made either in this country or abroad. Pick out the details that stick out most vividly in your mind and make notes covering the following areas before writing your account: sights; sounds; feelings; people you meet or see; atmosphere; unusual/funny/frightening experiences.
2. The next time you go away keep a diary of your experiences and write a detailed description of your trip concentrating only on details which will interest your readers.

Reading Modern Prose

Reading stories and novels should always be an enjoyable experience. It is important to be able to enter into the world of the story so that you can really become involved with the characters.

These pages are about getting more out of your reading of modern stories and novels.

Starting a book

Sometimes you have to work quite hard at the beginning of a book in order to become interested in what is going on. It is useful to ask yourself the following questions when you start a new book or story. This will help you to understand what the writer wants you to feel or think about.

- Where is the story set?
- What do you find out about the characters you meet?
- Are you meant to like the characters?
- What sort of story do you think it is going to be, for example, a love story, thriller, war story, science fiction, ghost story, etc.?
- What do you think is going to happen next?
- How is the writer trying to get you interested in the story?

Read the opening to the novel *Aliens in the Family* by the New Zealand writer Margaret Mahy and think about the above questions.

Even the most ordinary of days can be full of secrets and mysteries, and this particular Thursday was no exception. It was full of people, setting off from certain places and arriving at others. Thursday's children have far to go ...

Jacqueline Raven was not only travelling on a Thursday, she had been born on a Thursday too. She was setting out from a small country airport to visit her father, whom she had not seen for over a year. Since she had last seen him he had married again and now had a new family that Jacqueline had never met. Her own life had changed too, so much so in fact that she found it hard to believe that the girl she had once been had ever existed. She was sure the new family would not like her, and was quite certain that she would not like them, but there was no way around it. If she wanted to see her father again she would have to see them too, for the new children belonged to him more than she did these days, and she must try hard to accept them and like them. Not that this was her only problem. She did not feel at all comfortable about leaving Pet, her mother.

'Don't forget?' she said, turning anxiously to Pet, 'if Granny can't sleep and starts getting up in the night and tidying drawers, that little blue pill is the one to give her. It just makes her restful and ...'

'Don't worry, dear!' said Pet. 'I won't forget.' But Jacqueline, who really preferred to be called Jake, knew her mother often did forget such things, and although she was always sorry afterwards, afterwards was usually too late.

Different plots

Many modern novels have more than one plot to keep the readers interested. In *Aliens in the Family* we are quickly introduced to another main character in a different world altogether.

When you start a new book it is a good idea to keep a journal so that you can note down important ideas in each chapter. You may find that your feelings and understanding will change as you get further into the book.

Short Stories and Novels

While Jake was saying goodbye to her mother, and in the city far away her new relations were arguing about the sort of thing that might make her feel at home, a farewell of a very different sort was about to take place in a different space and time from her own.

Bond was walking confidently along the rounded corridor of his school – the only home he had ever known. He was the only one awake in the dormitory and the dreams of his fellow students fretted the edge of his thoughts like a cloud of rainbow gnats, staining his vision with their colours ...

His school could flick through the dimensions of space as easily as a cat takes short cuts through back gardens. It could swing round whole planetary systems gathering in enough of their energy to hurl itself outwards on vast journeys, not only through space but back in time as well.

from *Aliens in the Family* by Margaret May

One of the most enjoyable things when reading a book is to see what happens when the different characters come into contact with each other and how the different plots link up.

summary

When you read a novel or a story keep a journal in which you can record your thoughts about the following:

- **Characters** — Do you like/dislike them?
  — Do they change as the story develops?
- **Plot** — Is it realistic?
  — Do things turn out as you expected?
- **Style** — Is the book easy to understand?
  — Is the language difficult/exciting/unusual?

Questions

A

1. Name four different types of story that you will commonly come across.
2. Why is it a good idea to keep a journal when reading a novel or a story?
3. In the opening to *Aliens in the Family* where is Jacqueline Raven going?
4. What is her mother's name?
5. What does Jacqueline tell her mother not to forget?

B

1. Do you think Jacqueline is looking forward to seeing her father? Give reasons for your answer.
2. What are the different things you have learnt about Jacqueline in the opening of the book?
3. In the second extract what do you find out about Bond?
4. What sort of book do you think *Aliens in the Family* will be?
5. What clues does the title of the book give you as to what might happen?

C

1. Write your own version of what happens when Jacqueline meets her father and his new family.
2. Write a journal entry for a book (story or novel) you are reading at the moment. Include details about what you have found out already, what the main characters are like, what you think the story is about and what you think is going to happen. You can include drawings, diagrams, maps, cartoons, etc. to illustrate the story if you like.

103

Reading Older Prose

intro

When you read a story or a novel that was written over a hundred years ago you will notice a lot of things that are very different from the stories that are written today.

These pages are about helping you to enjoy reading older novels and stories.

Events in the past

The way people live has changed greatly and so descriptions of people and their lifestyles will be quite different in older books – there will be no mention of telephones or televisions or computers for example!

Also town and country life has changed a great deal since 1900 – there will be no mention of cars or airports or housing estates.

Language change

Language is another thing that changes very quickly from generation to generation, so when you read an older book you will come across a lot of unusual words and expressions which you may have to look up in a dictionary.

Reading an older novel or story will often give you a fascinating picture of what it was like to live in previous centuries. It will also show you that in many ways people's emotions were exactly the same as today with the same hopes and fears and dreams.

Read the following extract from a short story by the famous nineteenth-century writer Thomas Hardy. In this story a boy has his horse stolen by thieves on Christmas Eve as he is returning home from town. He stumbles upon a large house and discovers the same thieves making plans to rob it. He decides to tell the owners of the house what he has found out, but he has to interrupt a dinner party.

'Hullo! What disturbance are you making here?' said a footman who opened the door; and, seizing Hubert by the shoulder, he pulled him into the dining-hall. 'Here's a strange boy I have found making a noise in the porch, Sir Simon.'
Everybody turned.

'Bring him forward,' said Sir Simon, the old gentleman before mentioned. 'What were you doing there, my boy?'
'Why, his arms are tied!' said one of the ladies.
'Poor fellow!' said another.
Hubert at once began to explain that he had been waylaid on his journey home, robbed of his horse, and mercilessly left in this condition by the thieves.
'Only to think of it!' exclaimed Sir Simon.
'That's a likely story,' said one of the gentleman guests, incredulously.

'Doubtful, hey?' asked Sir Simon.

'Perhaps he's a robber himself,' suggested a lady.

'There is a curiously wild wicked look about him, certainly, now that I examine him closely,' said the old mother. Hubert blushed with shame; and, instead of continuing his story, and relating that robbers were concealed in the house, he doggedly held his tongue, and half resolved to let them find out their danger for themselves.

'Well, untie him,' said Sir Simon. 'Come, since it is Christmas Eve, we'll treat him well. Here my lad; sit down in that empty seat at the bottom of the table, and make as good a meal as you can. When you have had your fill we will listen to more particulars of your story.'

After a little while Hubert thinks up a clever plan to reveal where the thieves are hiding.

'Tell the ladies who you are, what you are made of, and what you can do,' the young man continued, slapping Hubert upon the shoulder.

'Certainly,' said our hero, drawing himself up, and thinking it best to put a bold face on the matter. 'I am a travelling magician.'

'Indeed!'

'What shall we hear next?'

'Can you call up spirits from the vasty deep, young wizard?'

'I can conjure up a tempest in a cupboard,' Hubert replied.

'Ha-Ha!' said the old Baronet, pleasantly rubbing his hands. 'We must see this performance. Girls, don't go away: here's something to be seen.'

'Not dangerous, I hope?' said the old lady.

Hubert rose from the table. 'Hand me your snuff-box, please,' he said to the young man who had made free with him. 'And now,' he continued, 'without the least noise, follow me. If any of you speak it will break the spell.'

from *The Thieves Who Couldn't Help Sneezing* by Thomas Hardy

Draw a table with headings and note down all the different things in this extract which tell you that it was written over one hundred years ago. Some ideas for your headings could be: unusual words; the way people speak; customs and habits; punctuation. Try and think of some headings of your own.

Summary

Once you get used to the different styles of writing and unusual language you will find older novels and stories just as interesting as modern ones.

When you read a pre-twentieth-century story or novel:
- check the meanings of unfamiliar words
- note down what you find out about differences in the way people lived and behaved
- find out what you can about life in the time when the book was written.

Questions

A

Write down five things which will tell you that this story was written over a hundred years ago. Explain the reasons for each of your choices.

B

1. In the first extract how do the guests react to the appearance of Hubert? Do they all react in the same way?
2. Why do you think Hubert does not tell them about the thieves hiding in the house?
3. What sort of a person is Sir Simon? Are we meant to like him?
4. What do you think Hubert's plan is? How might this link up with the title of the story?
5. Imagine you could talk to the boy about the events of this night. Write the conversation you have with him where he tells you what happened.

C

Continue the story in your own way, trying to keep to the same style as the original.

F

Thomas Hardy is very well known for his novels which are set in the South West of England and are about the lives of country people who come into contact with people from the towns. His most famous novels are *Far from the Madding Crowd* (1874), *The Mayor of Casterbridge* (1886) and *Tess of the d'Urbervilles* (1891). In later life he also wrote a great deal of poetry.

Myths

intro

Myths are old stories that were passed down by word of mouth for centuries before writing was invented. Over the years they changed and grew. They are about gods, humans and strange creatures. Although not 'true' in an everyday sense, they contain a meaning and wisdom of their own.

> These pages are about myths and tell the myth of the Greek hero Perseus.

The myth of Perseus

The birth of Perseus came about rather strangely. Zeus, father of the gods, had disguised himself as a shower of gold so that he could secretly visit a maiden imprisoned in a tower by her father. Her name was Danae. When she gave birth to Perseus, her father set her and the baby adrift on the sea. Luckily a fisherman found them and took them to King Polydectes, who looked after them both in his palace.

Perseus grew to be a brave young man. Polydectes now decided he wanted to marry Danae. Unfortunately she didn't like the idea much, and Perseus had to defend her against the king. Eventually Polydectes pretended he was going to marry someone else and sent Perseus off to fetch a wedding present.

This wasn't just any present – it was the head of the monster Medusa. She had snakes for hair, huge teeth and a dangling tongue. Not a pretty sight. In fact she was so ugly that anyone who saw her was turned to stone. However, Perseus had powerful allies. The goddess Athene gave him a shield polished mirror-bright. The god Hermes gave him a jewel sickle with which to cut off Medusa's head.

Perseus now needed some winged sandals, a magic wallet to hold the head, and a helmet with the power to make him invisible. These were all in the care of the Underworld Nymphs. However, to find out where these Nymphs lived, Perseus had to track down three monstrous sisters who had only one eye and one tooth between them. He snatched the eye and tooth and forced the sisters to tell him where to find the Nymphs.

Finally, fully equipped, Perseus found Medusa. With Athene's help, and using the shield as a mirror to avoid looking directly at Medusa, he cut off her head. Out of her body sprang the winged horse Pegasus. Stuffing the head in the wallet, Perseus mounted Pegasus and rode off into the sky.

Perseus flew to Egypt, stopping off only to turn an unfriendly giant into a mountain by showing him Medusa's head. Rounding the coast, he caught sight of a young woman chained to a sea cliff. He discovered from her parents – King Cepheus and Cassiopeia – that she was called Andromeda, and was to be sacrificed to a sea monster. Perseus agreed to rescue her on condition that she would be his wife.

True to his word, Perseus beheaded the monster and freed the grateful Andromeda. She married him at once, but now her parents turned against him. There was a fight, and of course out came the horrible head. Cepheus and Cassiopeia, and their supporters, were turned to stone.

Perseus took his new bride home to meet his mother, only to find that now King Polydectes was threatening her. When Perseus announced to the king that he was back with the wedding present, Polydectes laughed insultingly.

You can probably guess what happened next. Before you could say 'Medusa', Polydectes and friends had all been turned to garden ornaments! As for the fisherman who saved baby Perseus and his mother, Perseus made him king.

Short Stories and Novels

This is a picture of Medusa from an ancient Greek vase

H

The adjective from myth is **mythical**: Perseus is a mythical character. The subject or study of myths is called **mythology**. Many people use the word myth for anything commonly believed but untrue, for example, 'It is a myth that the black bit at the end of a banana is poisonous.'

summary

- Myths are ancient stories. They are not historically true, but they have a meaning.
- Perseus is a mythical hero. The son of Zeus, he protects his mother and cuts off Medusa's head.

Questions

A

1. Why did myths change and grow gradually?
2. What kinds of things are myths about?
3. What is the name of Perseus' mother?
4. Who helps Perseus to kill Medusa?
5. Who is Andromeda?

B

1. Divide the Perseus story into at least four episodes for a television series. Give each one a title.
2. Make a list of characters – human and otherwise – in the Perseus myth. Add brief notes on who or what each one is.
3. Imagine you are Perseus. Tell the story of how you killed Medusa. Remember that you had to walk backwards looking in the mirror. Athene guided your hand.
4. Tell the story from the point of view of Andromeda or Pegasus, from when they first set eyes on Perseus.

C

Make drawings with captions, or describe in words, your three most exciting scenes from the story.

For more information about old stories see pages 108–109

Legends

Legends are old stories. They are based on things that actually happened to real people, but over years of telling they have been changed and added to. They are different from myths (see pages 106–107), which are not based on real events.

> These pages are about legends and describe the legend of King Arthur, Queen Guinevere and Sir Lancelot.

King Arthur

One legendary figure is King Arthur. Many people think there was a historical Arthur who ruled the Britons after the Romans, and who won 12 victories against invaders between AD490 and AD500.

Stories tell how Arthur proved his right to be king by pulling a sword from a stone, and how he received help and advice from the magician Merlin. They also tell of his Knights of the Round Table, and his queen, Guinevere. No one knows how much truth there is in these stories.

Lancelot, Guinevere and the Sword Bridge

Lancelot was King Arthur's friend, a brave and honourable knight. Guinevere was Arthur's queen, and Lancelot was devoted to her. More than that, he loved her, and she loved him. Both were torn between their feelings for each other and their loyalty to Arthur. This love story could have no happy ending.

But there was another knight who claimed to love Guinevere: Prince Meliagante, son of the King of Gorre. Meliagante was an evil man, and one day he managed to capture Guinevere and some of her knights.

▶ *This illustration tells the story of Lancelot, Guinevere and the Sword Bridge*

Short Stories and Novels

When Lancelot heard, he was furious. He pursued Meliagante, but found that the kingdom was protected by a deep and dangerous river. To prove his love for Guinevere, he chose the hardest way across. This was the Sword Bridge, a huge sword spanning the river, its razor-sharp blade uppermost. To prove his love even more, Lancelot removed the armour from his hands and feet before crawling across.

Reaching the other side, Lancelot attacked the lions that stood on guard, but found that they were an illusion. Meliagante's father, the King of Gorre, was impressed. He tried to get his son to make peace, but Meliagante refused.

The next day, though terribly wounded from the Sword Bridge, Lancelot fought with Meliagante. They were evenly matched, and the battle was so long and fierce that the king begged Guinevere to stop it.

She called from the tower in which she was a prisoner, and Lancelot immediately stopped defending himself. Meliagante, on the other hand, kept up a rain of blows on Lancelot until servants held him back.

Guinevere and her knights were released on one condition – that Lancelot fight Meliagante again for her in a year and a day. Meanwhile, Meliagante imprisoned Lancelot in a tower without windows. He was still there when the year and a day had passed. Meliagante tried to convince Guinevere that Lancelot didn't love her anymore, but at the last minute Lancelot escaped.

Lancelot was exhausted, but the sight of his enemy enraged him. He threw himself on Meliagante, beat him down and killed him. Lancelot was a hero. Guinevere was saved.

summary

- Legends are old stories loosely based on real people and events. King Arthur is a legendary figure.
- Arthur's knight Lancelot loved Guinevere and rescued her when she was carried off by Prince Meliagante.

Questions

A

1. How are legends different from myths?
2. What shape was Arthur's famous table?
3. Why was the love between Lancelot and Guinevere doomed?
4. When and why did Lancelot remove some armour?

B

1. List the characters in the Sword Bridge story. Add brief notes on each character.
2. Write a diary entry for Lancelot or Guinevere for the day of Lancelot's first fight with Meliagante. Lancelot's could begin: 'Today was the hardest day of my life. I woke up, my hands and feet in bandages...'. Guinevere's could start: 'At last I've been freed from the tower...'.
3. Write a poem about Lancelot crossing the bridge. Remember the river, the sharp blade, the lions and the thought of Guinevere that kept him going.
4. Imagine you are
   (a) Meliagante watching Lancelot cross the bridge,
   (b) Guinevere imprisoned, or
   (c) Lancelot finally victorious.

   Describe your thoughts and feelings.

C

Explain your thoughts about how each character in the story behaves. For example, do you think Lancelot is right to obey Guinevere so quickly?

For more information about old stories see pages 106–107

Character Description

intro

In any work of fiction it is very important for the writer to create characters that readers will be interested in. Otherwise they will stop reading the book.

These pages are about the different ways of creating interesting characters in stories and novels.

Introducing characters

There are many different ways of introducing and describing characters in a story. Here are some of the commonest methods:

- **Dialogue**. When characters speak we can learn what they are thinking and feeling, as well as something about their personality. We might also find out from their accent and manner of speaking where they come from and something about their background.
- **Appearance**. This includes what characters look like, what they are wearing, how they move, etc.
- **Thoughts**. Some writers describe what is going on in the characters' minds so the reader learns about their thoughts, ideas and feelings.
- **Behaviour**. How characters act in a particular situation will tell the reader more about their personality.
- **Other people's comments and opinions**.

Physical appearance

Charles Dickens, the great nineteenth-century writer, is famous for his character descriptions. He often uses exaggerated description to make a character look ridiculous. Read the following extract from his novel *Hard Times* where he introduces the unpleasant, boastful character of Mr Bounderby.

He was a rich man: banker, merchant, manufacturer, and what not. A big, loud man, with a stare, and a metallic laugh. A man made out of a coarse material, which seemed to have been stretched to make so much of him. A man with a great puffed head and forehead, swelled veins in his temples, and such a strained skin to his face that it seemed to hold his eyes open, and lift his eyebrows up. A man with a pervading appearance on him of being inflated like a balloon, and ready to start. A man who could never sufficiently vaunt himself a self-made man. A man who was always proclaiming, through that brassy speaking-trumpet of a voice of his, his old ignorance and his old poverty. A man who was the Bully of humility ...

Short Stories and Novels

He had not much hair. One might have fancied he had talked it off; and that what was left, all standing up in disorder, was in that condition from being constantly blown about by his windy boastfulness.

from **Hard Times** by Charles Dickens

In this description Dickens uses the physical appearance of Bounderby to tell the reader about his personality.

Inside a character's head

Many writers like to describe what is going on inside a character's head — it is a good way of quickly getting the readers involved with the story.

The twentieth-century writer Graham Greene starts off his novel *A Gun for Sale* as if he knows what a hired killer might be thinking.

Murder didn't mean much to Raven. It was just a new job. You had to be careful. You had to use your brains. It was not a question of hatred. He had only seen the Minister once.

Greene then describes Raven's appearance and actions and gives some information about his background.

He carried an attaché case. He looked like any other youngish man going home after his work; his dark overcoat had a clerical air. He moved steadily up the street like hundreds of his kind. A tram went by, lit up in the early dusk: he didn't take it. An economical young man, you might have thought, saving money for his home. Perhaps even now he was on his way to meet his girl.

H

The description of Bounderby by Dickens is an example of caricature. This is where the appearance of a character is exaggerated to make the person look ridiculous. It is rather like drawing a cartoon. Dickens wants the readers to dislike Bounderby. To emphasise this even more, Dickens has deliberately used the word bounder, which is an old-fashioned word for a rude, loud-mouthed person, in the character's name.

For more information about descriptive words see pages 20–21

But Raven had never had a girl.

A little later, as Raven is about to commit the murder, Graham Greene describes the character's thoughts once more, to increase the tension.

Raven sat down and fixed his eyes on the Minister's chest. He thought: I'll give her three minutes by the alarm clock to get well away: he kept his eyes on the Minister's chest: just there I'll shoot.

from **A Gun for Sale** by Graham Greene

summary

- Writers use many different techniques to make characters interesting and believable. They also use the way they describe the characters to make the reader like or dislike them. It is important for the reader to know what the character is thinking and feeling as well as what they look like and what they do.

Questions

A

1. Name four different ways of introducing a character into a story or novel.
2. What is caricature and why will a writer use it?
3. What words in the first extract tell us that Dickens does not want the reader to like the character of Bounderby?

B

1. Read the first extract again. In your own words describe what Bounderby looks like.
2. What different techniques does Graham Greene use to introduce the character of Raven? How effective are they? Give your reasons.
3. What different things do we learn about Raven? Why do you think the author chose this particular name for him?

C

1. Imagine that you could ask Mr Bounderby some questions about his life. Write an interview with him giving him an opportunity to talk about himself and his background.
2. Write the opening to a story where you introduce two characters. Use two different techniques to describe them.

Plot and Theme

intro

The **plot** of a story or novel consists of the different things that happen to the characters which move the story along from beginning to end. The **theme** is what all these events tell us about the characters and what the main ideas of the story are.

> These pages are about the importance of the plot in a story and how to look out for themes.

How a plot works

Most novels and stories start off with an introduction to the main characters and then move on to some sort of problem or conflict which affects them. For example, in a detective story someone might get killed; in a love story a relationship might break up; in a horror story someone might get attacked.

The next stage of the story shows how the characters deal with these problems.

Depending on what happens to the characters the ending is either happy or sad or will contain perhaps a mixture of different emotions.

Recognising the themes

The theme of a story is what the writer wants you to think about as you read the book. So in a war story, for example, the writer might want you to think about why wars start and the waste of life involved. A love story might make you think about why relationships can sometimes be very complicated.

To understand the theme you need to think about the characters and the way they behave in certain situations.

Careful reading

In the novel *Goodnight Mr Tom* by the modern writer Michelle Magorian, a young boy is evacuated from London before the start of the Second World War. He is sent to stay with an old man, Thomas Oakley, who is thought of as being gruff and unsociable. The opening chapter of the book introduces us to the two main characters and quickly presents some of the problems they will face.

Willie pulled a small wooden stool from a corner and sat down in front of the fire. He felt frightened and lonely.

'What you got in yer bag, then?'

'I dunno,' mumbled Willie, 'Mum packed it. She said I weren't to look in.' One of his socks slid half-way down his leg, revealing a large multicoloured bruise on his shin and a swollen red sore beside.

'That's a nasty ole thing,' Tom said, pointing to it. 'What give you that?' Willie paled and pulled the sock up quickly.

'Best drink that afore it gits cold,' said Tom, sensing that the subject needed to be changed. Willie looked intently at the changing shapes of the flames in the fire and slowly drank the tea. It thundered in his throat in his attempt to swallow it quietly. Tom left the room briefly and within a few minutes returned.

'I gotta go out for a spell …

Willie heard him slam the front door and listened to the sound of his footsteps gradually fading. He hugged himself tightly and rocked backwards and forwards on the stool. 'I must be good,' he whispered urgently, 'I must be good,' and he rubbed a sore spot on his arm. He was such a bad boy, he knew that. Mum said she was kinder to him than most mothers. She only gave him soft beatings. He shuddered. He was dreading the moment when Mr Oakley would discover how wicked he was. He was stronger-looking than Mum.

A little later, in the second chapter, Tom opens the bag that Willie has brought with him from home.

There was one small towel, a piece of soap, a toothbrush, an old Bible, and an envelope with 'To whom it may concern' written on it. He looked under the towel for some night clothes but there were none.

Short Stories and Novels

summary

- When you read a story look out for the way the writer tries to make the plot interesting. Some plots are very straightforward while others might be extremely complicated with lots of different plots merging together.
- The plot will give you an idea about the theme or themes of the book – this is what the writer wants you to think about as you are reading.

He opened the envelope. Willie heard the paper being torn and turned to watch him. He knew the letter was from his Mum. He checked again that his socks were pulled up and stood very still.

'Dear Sir or Madam,' it read, 'I asked if Willie could go and stay with God-fearing people so I hope he is. Like most boys he's full of sin but he's promised to be good. I can't visit him. I'm a widow and I haven't got the money. The war and that. I've put the belt in for when he's bad and I've sewn him in for the winter. I usually keep him in when I wash his clothes and I got them special for the cold weather so he should be alright. Tell him his mother said he'd better be good. Mrs. Beech.'

Tom folded the letter and put it into his pocket. He found the belt at the bottom of the bag. It was a brown leather one with a steel buckle. He put it back in the bag and took out the towel, soap and toothbrush. Willie stood with his back to the fire and stared uneasily up at him.

Tom was angry.

from *Goodnight Mr Tom* by Michelle Magorian

Goodnight Mr Tom is a full-length novel so there are many twists and turns to the plot with several different problems affecting a variety of characters. This keeps the reader interested and wanting to read on.

There are also several themes to the book including: education and growing up, friendship, the experience of death, family life.

For more information about reading a story see pages 102–103

Questions

A

1. What is meant by the plot of a story or novel?
2. What do we mean when we talk about the theme or themes of a book?
3. In the first extract from *Goodnight Mr Tom* what does Tom do to make Willie feel more comfortable?
4. What does Willie do when Tom notices the bruise on his leg?

B

1. How is Willie feeling throughout these extracts?
2. How do you think Tom might be feeling about Willie staying with him for several months?
3. What can you tell about the relationship between Willie and his mother?
4. Why do you think Tom is angry at the end of the second extract?
5. How do you think the story might continue? Do you think it is going to be a happy story or a sad one? Give reasons for your answer.

C

1. From what you have read write down the plot details for the opening to *Goodnight Mr Tom*. Now write down what you would put in the plot for the rest of the book. (If you already know the story, make up an alternative.)
2. Write the plot for a war story set in the future. You will need to make brief notes about the main characters and what happens to them. What will the theme of your story be? Will the message of the book be that war is a terrible waste of life? Or will it be about bravery and struggling against danger?

Setting and Atmosphere

intro

Setting the scene is very important in a story or novel so the readers can imagine the place where the events are happening.

These pages are about why the setting of a story is important and how writers use the setting to create an atmosphere.

Setting the scene

The **setting** for a story might include the following features:

- the place where it happens
- the time in which it is set
  (in the present, the past or the future)
- the time of day
- the time of year
- the weather.

Many writers use the setting to create a certain **atmosphere** which is important for the rest of the story. A horror story, for example, might be set in a lonely house on a dark and stormy night.

In Robert Westall's novel *The Kingdom by the Sea* the author quickly gives the readers information about where and when the story is set. He does this at the same time as introducing the main character and starting the plot. By doing this the reader is drawn into the world of the story and wants to read on.

He was an old hand at air raids now.

As the yell of the siren climbed the sky, he came smoothly out of his dreams. Not scared. Only his stomach clamped down tight for action, as his hands found his clothes laid ready in the dark. Hauled one jumper, then another, over his pyjamas. Thrust both stockinged feet together through his trousers and into his shoes, then bent to tie his laces thoroughly. A loose lace had tripped him once, in the race to the shelter. He remembered the smashing blow as the ground hit his chin; the painful week after, not able to eat with a bitten tongue.

He grabbed his school raincoat off the door, pulling the door wide at the same time. All done by feel; no need to put the light on. Lights were dangerous.

He passed Dulcie's door, heard Mam and Dulcie muttering to each other, Dulcie sleepy and cross, Mam sharp and urgent. Then he thundered downstairs; the crack of light from the kitchen door lighting up the edge of each stair-tread. Dad was sitting in his warden's uniform, hauling on his big, black boots, his grey hair standing up vertically in a bunch, like a cock's comb. Without looking up, Dad said, 'Bloody Hitler! Four bloody nights in a row!'

from ***The Kingdom by the Sea*** by Robert Westall

What the setting tells you

When you start a new book look out for the clues which tell you about the setting. In the extract above what do you find out about where and when the story is set?

If you keep a reading journal, you can note down at the start of a book what you find out about the setting and what the atmosphere is like. This will help to prepare you for what is to come in the rest of the book. Some writers like to create the setting and the atmosphere before the plot begins, to give the readers time to get in the mood for the story. Charles Dickens does this in his novel *Bleak House*. This is a long novel about a legal case that becomes more and more confusing for the characters in the book. Dickens was criticising the law courts for making it impossible to find out the truth. In his opening to the book he wants to set a scene which is suitable for the events which are to follow.

H

Notice how Dickens uses many specialised words, like *caboose*, *collier-brigs* and *gunwales*, to do with boats and the river to make the setting detailed and realistic. You may need to look up these words in a dictionary.

Short Stories and Novels

Fog everywhere. Fog up the river, where it flows among green aits and meadows; fog down the river, where it rolls defiled among the tiers of shipping, and the waterside pollutions of a great (and dirty) city. Fog on the Essex marshes, fog on the Kentish heights. Fog creeping into the cabooses of collier brigs, fog lying out on the yards, and hovering in the rigging of great ships; fog drooping on the gunwales of barges and small boats. Fog in the eyes and throats of ancient Greenwich pensioners, wheezing by the firesides of their wards; fog in the stem and bowl of the afternoon pipe of the wrathful skipper, down in his close cabin, fog cruelly pinching the toes and fingers of his shivering little 'prentice boy on deck. Chance people on the bridges peeping over the parapets into a nether sky of fog, with fog all around them, as if they were up in a balloon, and hanging in the misty clouds.

from *Bleak House* by Charles Dickins

summary

- The setting of a story prepares you for what is to come and should get you interested in the book.
- A writer will try to create an atmosphere in the setting which is suitable for the events of the story.

Questions

A

1. Name four different things that a writer might describe in the setting of a book.
2. Why is the setting of a book important?
3. What is the atmosphere in the first extract?
4. In the second extract how many times is the word 'fog' mentioned?

B

1. In the first extract what can you tell from the setting about:
   a) the time of day?
   b) when the story is set; in the past, present or future?
   c) the feelings of the main character?
2. Write a letter from the boy in the first extract to a friend in another part of the country, telling him what it is like where he lives when the air raids start.

3. If you could interview Charles Dickens, what questions would you ask him about why he chose this opening to his novel? Write the answers that you think he would give you.

C

Write the opening page of a story in which you create a certain atmosphere and set the scene. Choose from the following categories: horror story; war story; love story; science fiction story; adventure story.

For more information on reading journals see pages 102–103

Narrative Technique and the Author's Voice

> These pages are about helping you to understand the different techniques a writer might use in a story and why the author's voice is important.

intro

Every writer uses different narrative techniques to get readers interested in a story. Some writers use dialogue (where characters speak to one another), to make the characters come alive; some use description to help the reader imagine the setting and the atmosphere; some writers use action scenes to move the story along quickly while other writers prefer to build the story up slowly.

Getting the reader interested

Read the following extract from a story by the twentieth-century American writer, Ernest Hemingway. What techniques do you think Hemingway is using? In this extract a doctor and his son are visiting a native Indian camp in North America. The doctor has been called out to help a woman give birth to her baby.

Inside on a wooden bunk lay a young Indian woman. She had been trying to have her baby for two days. All the old women in the camp had been helping her. The men had moved off up the road to sit in the dark and smoke out of range of the noise she made. She screamed just as Nick and the two Indians followed his father and Uncle George into the shanty. She lay in the lower bunk, very big under a quilt. Her head was turned to one side. In the upper bunk was her husband. He had cut his foot very badly with an axe three days before. He was smoking a pipe. The room smelled very bad.

Nick's father ordered some water to be put on the stove, and while it was heating he spoke to Nick.

'This lady is going to have a baby, Nick,' he said.

'I know,' said Nick.

'You don't know,' said his father. 'Listen to me. What she is going through is called being in labour. The baby wants to be born and she wants it to be born. All her muscles are trying to get the baby born. That is what is happening when she screams.'

'I see,' Nick said.

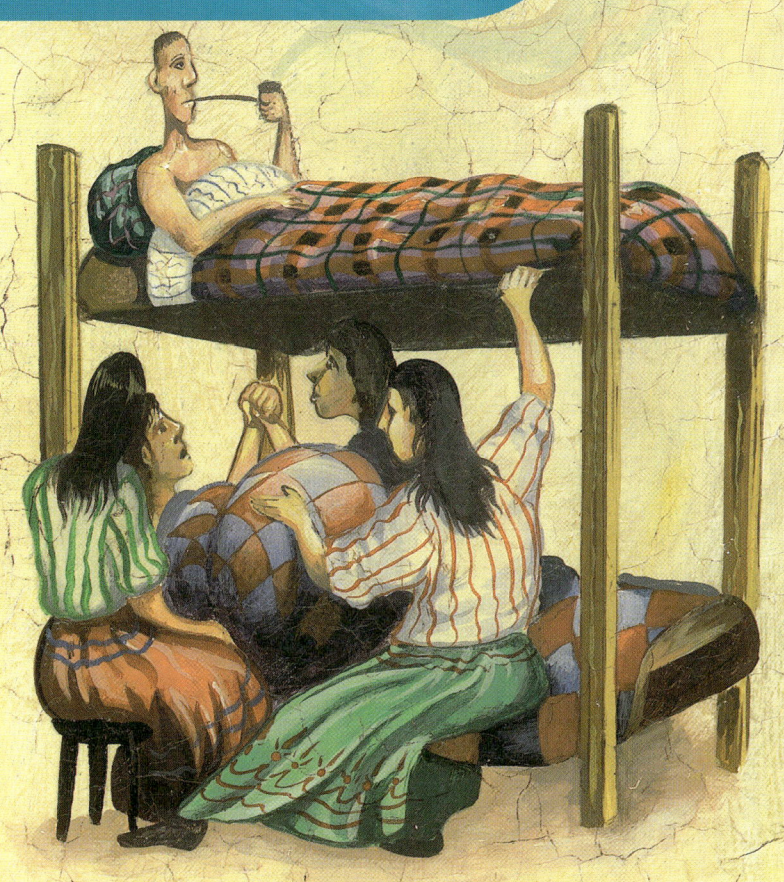

Just then the woman cried out.

'Oh, Daddy, can't you give her something to make her stop screaming?' asked Nick. 'No, I haven't any anaesthetic,' his father said.

'Indian Camp' from **The Snows of Kilimanjaro** by Ernest Hemingway

One of the techniques which Hemingway uses is to write in very short sentences rather like a newspaper report. (Hemingway was in fact a journalist.) This makes the story move quickly and creates tension.

Short Stories and Novels

Another technique is to leave out any description of the characters' feelings so the readers have to work out what they are feeling from the dialogue.

H

Other narrative techniques include:
flashbacks – where the story goes back in time, perhaps through a character's memory and where the events of the story do not follow a normal time sequence **letters and diaries** – these can bring out a character's feelings very effectively **mixed first and third person narrative** – the writer can tell the story from different points of view **cliffhangers** – where something very dramatic happens at the end of every chapter to make you want to read on.

Author's voice

The above extract is an example of **third person narrative**. This means the author is describing the events as if he is looking on from the outside.

Another way of writing that authors use is the **first person narrative**. This is when the events are narrated by one of the characters actually taking part in the story. For example, Anne Fine starts off her novel, *The Book of the Banshee*, like this:

Today a writer came to school and gave a talk to our class and 3b... Chopper thought she was a new teacher, so he took an interest. I pointed out that she couldn't have come for an interview, the bag on the floor beside her was too full. And she couldn't have come to start teaching, either. No one turns up at lunch time on their first day.

from *The Book of the Banshee* by Anne Fine

The first person narrative technique makes the writing very lively and fresh because it seems as if the character in the story is standing next to us having a conversation. We can believe in the reality of this person very quickly. Another way the author helps us to believe in the character is by having him use slang and humorous language which makes us feel on familiar terms with him.

First person narrative helps us to get closer to one particular character. Third person narrative helps us to get an overview of all the characters and what happens to them.

summary

- It is useful to recognise the narrative techniques a writer uses as this will help you to understand what the writer wants you to feel and think about as you read the book.
- First person narrative is where the story is told by one of the characters in the book. We see everything through this person's eyes.
- Third person narrative is where the story is told by the writer looking on at all the events from the outside.

Questions

A

1. Give three examples of narrative technique.
2. What is first person narrative?
3. What is third person narrative?

B

1. Do you think the short sentences are effective in the first extract? Do they help to make the story dramatic? Give reasons for your answers.
2. What are the advantages and disadvantages of writing a story: (a) in the first person, and (b) in the third person?
3. Which of these extracts do you prefer and why? Is it anything to do with the narrative techniques involved?
4. When you write a story do you like to use the first person narrative or the third? Why?

C

1. Re-write the extract from *Indian Camp* telling the story from the point of view of either the boy or the Indian woman.
2. Write two openings to a horror story, one using a first person narrative and the second using a third person narrative. When you have written them answer these questions.
a) Which one was easier to write or were they about the same?
b) Which one did you prefer writing and why?
c) Which one do you think works better?

117

Writing Your Own Short Story

intro

When writing a story you need to think about how to make it interesting, and what you want your readers to feel when they read it.

These pages are about helping you to write your own stories.

Planning

When you want to write a story you will need to start off with a plan to help you make the most of your ideas and to make the story interesting for anyone who reads it.

In your plan it is a good idea to make some headings where you can note down the different ideas you have. Of course you may want to change these ideas later as the story develops. Your headings should include the following:

- **Plot and theme**
  What is going to happen in the story?
  What is it going to be about?
- **Characters**
  How many characters will there be? (You may not want to have too many characters or it might be confusing.) Is the reader meant to like/dislike them? Will they be realistic/fantasy/cartoons/animals?
- **Narrative**
  Will it be written in first or third person narrative? Is it going to be exciting/tense/descriptive? Do you want the readers to laugh or cry or be frightened?
- **Setting**
  Where and when will the story be set?

Drafting and revising

Using your plan you can now write the first draft of your story. This is an opportunity for you to try out different ideas and to experiment with words and style.

When you read over what you have written you can then make changes, crossing things out and adding other details according to what you want your story to do. After you have revised your story carefully, you will be able to write the final version.

Read the following opening to a story by the twentieth-century writer Dylan Thomas. Try to see what he has done to make the story lively and unusual.

In the middle of the night I woke from a dream full of whips and lariats as long as serpents, and runaway coaches on mountain passes, and wide, windy gallops over cactus fields, and I heard the man in the next room crying, 'Gee-up!' and 'Whoa!' and trotting his tongue on the roof of his mouth.

It was the first time I had stayed in grandpa's house. The floorboards had squeaked like mice as I climbed into bed, and the mice between the walls had creaked like wood as though another visitor was walking on them. It was a mild summer night, but curtains had flapped and branches beaten against the window. I had pulled the sheets over my head, and soon was roaring and riding in a book.

'Whoa there my beauties!' cried grandpa. His voice sounded very young and loud, and his tongue had powerful hooves, and he made his bedroom into a great meadow. I thought I would see if he was ill, or had set his bedclothes on fire, for my mother had said that he lit his pipe under the blankets, and had warned me to run to his help if I smelt smoke in the night. I went on tiptoe through the darkness to his bedroom door, brushing against the furniture and upsetting a candlestick with a thump.

When I saw there was a light in the room I felt frightened, and as I opened the door I heard grandpa shout, 'Gee-up!' as loudly as a bull with a megaphone.

He was sitting straight up in bed and rocking from side to side as though the bed were on a rough road; the knotted edges of the counterpane were his reins; his invisible horse stood in a shadow beyond the bedside candle. Over a white flannel nightshirt he was wearing a red waistcoat with walnut-sized brass buttons. The over-filled bowl of his pipe smouldered among his whiskers like a little burning hayrick on a stick. At the sight of me, his hands dropped from the reins and lay blue and quiet, the bed stopped still on a level road, he muffled his tongue into silence, and the horses drew softly up.

'Is there anything the matter, grandpa?' I asked, though the clothes were not on fire. His face in the candlelight looked like a ragged quilt pinned upright on the black air and patched all over with goat-beards.

Short Stories and Novels

> **H**
> Notice how Dylan Thomas has used a lot of unusual descriptive words to make the setting and the characters come alive.

summary
- Careful planning is essential when writing a story. You need to think about who your story is aimed at and how you want your readers to feel.
- Unusual and original description is often more important than a clever plot.

He stared at me mildly. Then he blew down his pipe, scattering the sparks and making a high, wet dog whistle of the stem, and shouted: 'Ask no questions.'

After a pause he said slyly: 'Do you ever have nightmares, boy?'

I said: 'No.'

'Oh yes, you do,' he said.

I said I was woken by a voice that was shouting to horses.

'What did I tell you?' he said. 'You eat too much. Who ever heard of horses in a bedroom?'

He fumbled under his pillow, brought out a small, tinkling bag and carefully untied its strings. He put a sovereign in my hand, and said: 'Buy a cake.' I thanked him and wished him good night.

As I closed my bedroom door, I heard his voice crying loudly and gaily.

from *A Visit to Grandpa's* by Dylan Thomas

Questions

A
1. Why is a plan important when writing a story?
2. What do you need to include in your plan?
3. Why is it a good idea to use original and unusual description in your story?
4. Why is it important to know who your story is aimed at?
5. After you have written your first draft what should you do with your story?

B
1. In the extract from *A Visit to Grandpa's* what is the setting?
2. Why do you think Dylan Thomas uses so much description at the beginning of this story?
3. This is an example of first person narrative. Do you think it is effective and why?
4. What do you think the writer wants us to feel when we read this story?

C
Write your own story about a visit to someone's house describing the place, the people you meet or stay with and the things that happen. Plan your story carefully and try to use unusual description. Write your first draft and then look over what you have written, changing words and phrases that are not interesting.

For more information about the techniques of stories see pages 110–117

Reading a Modern Poem

intro

Reading a poem takes a lot of practice. All poems need to be read out loud because the sound of the words is important to the meaning. (Originally poems were meant to be sung just like the songs you listen to today.) Even if you are not sure what a poem means, always try to listen out for the sounds and **rhythms**. The rhythm refers to the way the lines of the poem flow, for example, whether they are smooth or jerky, fast or slow.

These pages are about helping you to read modern poems with enjoyment and understanding.

Approaching the poem

Sometimes when you hear a song for the first time, you are not sure whether you like it or not. Then when you hear it again it grows on you. The same is true of poetry. If you read a poem several times, you will give it a chance to get through to you.

When you read a poem for the first time it is a good idea to note down your first reactions to it on a piece of paper:

- You might comment on certain words or lines that interest you or confuse you.
- You might refer to how the poem is set out, for example, in separate **stanzas** (often called verses) or in one continuous piece of writing
- Are the lines all the same length or are there short and long ones? Does it rhyme?
- Is it funny or serious, happy or sad, or perhaps a mixture?

Read the poem opposite by the modern Indian writer Sujata Bhatt and then note down your first impressions.

Reading the poem

The words the poet has chosen will tell you how to read the poem – long words, for example, will slow the poem down while short words will speed it up.

Try to listen to the voice of the woman in the poem – imagine you can hear her speaking. Many words are repeated in the poem and there are a lot of questions. How might the woman be asking these questions? Now read the poem again.

Poems

H

When reading a poem you might not pause at the end of every line; sometimes you need to let the lines flow into each other – look out for the commas and full stops to help you.

Whenever you read a poem think about these questions:
- Are there different ways of saying it?
- Which words will you say loudly and which more softly?
- Where will you pause?
- Where will you change your voice, for example, from happy to sad?
- What do you think is the main thing the poet wants to get across in the poem?

summary

Pink Shrimps and Guesses

Hey, are you there
already, already
am I your mother?

Today I tried
to imagine your nose,
your eyebrows,
the shape your legs will take.
Whether you'll climb trees easily,
whether you'll cry easily.

Today I wanted you
to talk to me.
Tell me what you want.
Tell me, because I don't know.
Give me a hint at least.
When I look at the sky
can you smell the birds?
When I slip does your heart
beat faster? Do you like
red peppers? When I hear the birds
can you taste the sun on their feathers?
Tell me what you want.
Shall we meet face to face
in nine months, shall we?
Or would you rather forget about it?
I want to ask you
how it feels in there.
Do you mind if I run,
what are you thinking,
do my dreams keep you awake,
do I taste good already,
can you trust me?

Pink Shrimps and Guesses
by Sujata Bhatt

Questions

A

1. When we talk about the rhythm of a poem what do we mean?
2. How many stanzas are there in 'Pink Shrimps and Guesses'?
3. Who is the person speaking in the poem?
4. Who is she speaking to?
5. How many questions are there in the poem?

B

1. Imagine you could talk to the woman in the poem. Ask her some questions about how she is feeling and write down what she says in reply.
2. Why do you think there are so many questions in this poem?
3. Which words are repeated in the poem? Why do you think the poet repeats them?
4. When you read this poem out loud what sort of rhythm does it have? Write detailed notes describing how you would read it – which lines you would read quickly, which slowly, where you would pause, etc.
5. Why do you think the poet has chosen this particular title for the poem? Choose an alternative title and say why you chose it.
6. Pick out your favourite line and say why you like it.

C

1. Write a reply from the unborn baby to the mother. What might the baby want to ask its mother? You can either write this as a poem, a letter, a speech or description.
2. Do you think the woman in the poem is going to be a good parent? What advice would you give her about how to bring up her child? Prepare an advice sheet for parents about the best ways to treat their children.

121

Reading an Older Poem

intro

Language is changing all the time, so when you come across an older poem do not be surprised to find words that you may not be familiar with. The first thing to do is to find out what any unusual words mean.

These pages are about understanding how older poems were written so that you can read them with confidence.

Reading the poem

The lines in many older poems follow a set pattern and this will help you to read them. One very common pattern is for all the lines to contain ten **syllables**. A syllable is a part of a word which contains a separate vowel sound, such as December which is made up of three syllables (De-cem-ber). Having a regular number of syllables gives the poem a strong rhythm which you should try to listen out for.

Many poets use rhyme schemes in their poems to help the rhythm even more.

Can you discover a rhyming pattern, i.e. does every line rhyme or every second line?

Just as you would do with a modern poem it is important to note down your first reactions after reading a poem, even if you find some of the lines difficult to understand.

Read the following poem by the nineteenth-century poet Robert Southey, and see if you can work out the patterns he uses to give the poem its sense of rhythm.

December

A wrinkled, crabbèd man they picture thee,
Old Winter, with a rugged beard as grey
As the long moss upon the apple-tree;
Blue-lipped, an ice-drop at thy sharp blue nose,
Close muffled up, and on thy dreary way
Plodding along through sleet and drifting snows.

They should have drawn thee by thy high-heaped
   hearth,
Old Winter! seated in thy great armed chair;
Watching the children at their Christmas mirth; –
Or circled by them as thy lips declare
Some merry jest, or tale of murder dire
Or troubled spirit that disturbs the night;
Pausing at times to rouse the smouldering fire,
Or taste the old October brown and bright.

December by Robert Southey

Poems

Looking more closely

As you read the poem try to work out which lines have a natural pause at the end and which lines run on into each other.

Make a note of words which rhyme at the end of lines. When you read the poem try to hear the rhyming sounds.

Practise reading the poem bringing out the sounds of the words and emphasising the rhythm.

H

A common feature of pre-twentieth-century English is the use of 'thou' and 'thee' for 'you' and 'thy' for 'your'.

If a letter has a **stress mark** over it, for example, crabbèd, this means it is pronounced as a separate syllable – crabb-ed.

Make a list of the different pictures of December that the poet creates for the reader. Now read the poem again listening to the sounds and trying to imagine the pictures.

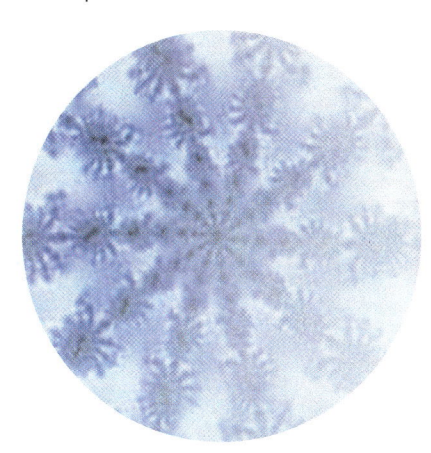

summary

When you read an older poem:
- try to follow the rhythm of the lines
- do not pause at the end of a line if it interrupts the flow of the words
- listen out for rhyming words
- read the poem several times before trying to have a clear idea of the meaning.

Questions

A

1. How many syllables are there in each line of the poem 'December'?
2. Does the poem rhyme?
3. Which lines rhyme?
4. How many colour words can you find in the poem?
5. Explain the meaning of 'crabbèd' as used in the poem.

B

1. How does the poet describe Winter in the first stanza? How does this picture change in the second stanza?
2. Which image of winter do you prefer and why?
3. Why do you think the poet compares Winter to an old man? Pick out all the words and phrases that describe what this old man looks like and is feeling.
4. How do you think this poem should be read out – in a happy way or sadly or perhaps with a mixture of feelings? Give reasons for your answer.

C

1. You have been asked to read this poem on the radio in a special programme about the seasons. Make detailed notes about how you are going to make the poem sound as effective as possible. Where will you pause, which words will you stress, how will you bring out different feelings, where will you lower and raise your voice? When you have made your notes make a tape-recording of your reading.
2. Write your own poem about another of the seasons or about a particular month comparing it to a person as Southey does in 'December'.

123

Sounds and Images

intro

Imagery is another name for the pictures that poets use to make a poem interesting and colourful. An image helps you to see and hear what is going on in the poem. Images also help you to feel the emotions that the poet wants to convey.

> These pages are about why poets use images and why the sound of words is important in poetry.

Types of imagery

Two very common types of imagery are **similes** and **metaphors**. A simile is where the poet compares one thing to another, for example, 'The wind tapped *like a tired man*' (Emily Dickinson).

A metaphor is where the poet is again making a comparison but this time without the use of the words *like* or *as*. For example, 'the Sun *is an orange dinghy*/sailing across a calm sea' (Wes Magee).

Why do you think poets use similes and metaphors?

Sound effects

Poets often use sounds to make a more vivid picture. If a poet uses words like crash, rustle, screech, this is called **onomatopoeia**. This is a Greek word and refers to words that have the same sound as their meaning.

Another common sound effect that you will find in many poems is **alliteration**. This is where the poet uses two or more words close together that start with the same letter, in order to emphasise a particular sound, such as '*by* the *bang* of *blood* in the *brain*' (Ted Hughes). All these 'b' sounds produce a heavy, thumping sound which is just right for the feeling of blood rushing round your head if you are frightened, for example.

Read the following poem by the modern Jamaican-born poet, James Berry. As you read, look and listen out for examples of imagery and sound effects.

> **H**
>
> James Berry has used imagery to make the wind seem human in places – this is called **personification**. (Robert Southey uses the same technique in his poem, 'December' – see pages 122–123.) This way he helps us to get more interested in what the wind is doing.

124

Poems

Workings of the Wind

Wind doesn't always topple trees and
shake houses to pieces

Wind plays all over woods, with weighty ghosts
in swings in thousands,
swinging from every branch.

Wind doesn't always rattle windows
and push, push at walls.

Wind whistles
down cul-de-sacs and worries
dry leaves and old newspapers to leap
and curl like kite tails.

Wind doesn't always dry out
sweaty shirts and blouses.

Wind scatters
pollen dust of flowers, washes
people's and animals' faces
and combs out birds' feathers.

Wind doesn't always whip up waves
into white horses.

Wind shakes up
tree shadows to dance on rivers,
to jig about on grass, and banging
lantern light to play signalman.

Wind doesn't always run wild
kicking tinny dustbin lids.

Wind makes
leafy limbs bow to red roses
and bob up and down outside windows
and makes desk papers fly up indoors.

Workings of the Wind by James Berry

For more information on personification see pages 130–131

Summary

- Poets use imagery to give us a clear picture of what is happening in the poem.
- Imagery also helps us to feel the emotions in the poem. The best way for a poet to encourage us to feel something is through imagery.
- Sound effects like alliteration and onomatopoeia are used to emphasise certain sounds and therefore to bring out the meaning and the feelings in the poem.

Questions

A

1. How many similes can you find in the poem?
2. How many metaphors can you find?
3. What examples of alliteration can you find?
4. Which letter sounds has James Berry chosen to emphasise?
5. What does onomatopoeia mean? Find some examples in the poem.

B

1. How is the poem set out? (Is there a pattern to the way the stanzas are arranged?)
2. What aspect of the wind does the poet describe in the two-line stanzas?
3. How does this contrast with the way he describes the wind in the four-line stanzas?
4. Look at the first line of each four-line stanza. Make a list of the things the wind does.
5. Do you think the poet likes the wind or not? Give reasons for your answer.

C

The poet uses several different images to describe the wind in this poem. Write a short essay about what this poem is about and how the images are used to bring out the meaning.

Rhyme and Rhythm

> These pages are about why rhythm is very important in a poem and why poets might use rhyme.

intro

All poems were originally sung, so the rhythm of the lines was obviously very important. If you hear a song with a lively, catchy sound, you are more likely to remember it. The same is true of poetry. Rhythm makes the lines more memorable and striking.

Why rhyme?

One way of helping to create a lively rhythm is to use **rhyme**. This stresses the sounds of words at the end of each line as well as emphasising their meaning. Various rhyme schemes can be used to create many different rhythmic effects. Look at the following opening to a well-known poem 'Night Mail' by the poet W. H. Auden.

This is the night mail crossing the border,
Bringing the cheque and the postal order,
Letters for the rich, letters for the poor,
The shop at the corner and the girl next door.

from **Night Mail** by W.H. Auden

The rhyme scheme is regular with each pair of lines rhyming. This is called **rhyming couplets**. It gives the poem a steady rhythm imitating the movement of the train.

What else does Auden do to help the rhythm in these lines? Look at the number of syllables in each line and the repetition of certain words.

Not all rhyme is so obvious and many poets do not use rhyme at all. Some poets use **half rhyme** where the rhyming sounds are similar but not identical. In the opening to the poem 'Blackberry-Picking' by Seamus Heaney, there is a mixture of half rhyme and full rhyme.

Late August, given heavy rain and sun
For a full week, the blackberries would ripen

> Half rhyme

At first, just one, a glossy purple clot
Among others, red, green, hard as a knot

> Full rhyme

from **Blackberry Picking** by Seamus Heaney

The rhythm here is quite different from 'Night Mail' even though the number of syllables in each line is virtually the same. How are the lines different?

Look at the way lines run into each other.
Look at the length of the words in each extract.

Catching the rhythm

The seventeenth-century poet Robert Herrick wrote the following poem about witchcraft. He created a striking rhythm. Read it out loud and listen to the flow of the lines.

> **H**
>
> Seventeenth-century spelling is different to our own in some cases, for example, 'Devill and shee'. You will notice too that many of the nouns are written with a capital letter.
>
> Also some words are shortened to keep the rhythm flowing, such as 'ne'r' for never and 'O'er' for over.

The Hag

The Hag is astride
This night for to ride;
The Devill and shee together:
Through thick and through thin,
Now out, and then in,
Though ne'r so foule be the weather.

A Thorn or a Burr
She takes for a Spurre:
With a lash of a Bramble she rides now,
Through Brakes and through Bryars
O'er Ditches and Mires,
She follows the Spirit that guides now.

No Beast, for his food,
Dares now range the wood;
But husht in his laire he lies lurking:
While mischiefs, by these,
On Land and on Seas,
At noone of Night are a working.

The storme will arise,
And trouble the skies;
This night, and more for the wonder,
The ghost from the Tomb
Affrighted shall come
Cal'd out by the clap of the Thunder.

The Hag
by Robert Herrick

Summary

- Rhythm is very important in poetry. It can be fast or slow, smooth or jerky, depending on the subject of the poem.
- Rhyme is one of the ways poets can help to create a strong sense of rhythm. There are many different rhyme patterns. Rhyme also emphasises the meaning and the themes of the poem.
- Poets might use full rhyme or half rhyme. Many poets do not use rhyme at all but all poems should have rhythm.

Questions

A

1. Why is rhythm important in a poem?
2. What is the difference between half rhyme and full rhyme?
3. What are rhyming couplets?
4. What is the rhyming pattern in the poem 'The Hag'?
5. How are the stanzas in 'The Hag' divided into short and long lines?

B

1. What are the different ways in which Robert Herrick creates the rhythm in 'The Hag'?
2. How do the length of the lines and the number of syllables affect the sound of the poem and the way it should be read?
3. Why do you think Robert Herrick uses rhyme in this poem?
4. Robert Herrick uses other sound effects like alliteration and onomatopoeia in this poem? Why do you think he does this?
5. Do you think the rhythm of the poem suits the subject matter? Explain why.

C

1. Collect six poems from your school library which have different rhythms. For each one, imagine that you were going to set the poem to music. Describe the sound that your poem would have and whether it would be lively or slow.
2. Collect six different examples of rhyming poems. How many different rhyming patterns can you find?

Writing About a Poem

intro

When you first read a poem you may not have a clear idea about its meaning, but there are always a lot of things you can say about the language and the layout of the poem. This is a very good starting point. The more you look at the language in the poem the more you will understand what the poet wants to say.

These pages are about the sort of things you need to look for when writing about a poem.

Writing about language and layout

It is a good idea to make a list of the different things you need to look out for in a poem. This list should include the following:

- **Layout**
  Is the poem in separate stanzas?
  Are the stanzas the same length?
  Are the lines long or short or a mixture?
- **Rhythm**
  Do the lines flow smoothly or are they jerky?
  Has the poet used long words to slow the poem down or short words to give a fast rhythm? Are there many punctuation marks that break up the flow of the words?
- **Rhyme**
  Has the poet used rhyme and what sort of rhyme?
  What is the rhyme pattern?
- **Alliteration**
  If alliteration is used, which letters are being emphasised?
- **Imagery**
  Are there similes and metaphors in the poem?
  What pictures do they help to make in your mind?
- **Diction** – the type of words that a poet uses.
  Some poets use very descriptive words, some use ordinary, everyday words.
- **Mood**
  Do the words and pictures in the poem make you feel happy or sad, angry or frightened?
- **Tone**
  Is the poem funny or serious or quietly thoughtful?

As you can see, there are a lot of things you can write about even if you are not quite sure of the meaning.

When you have read the poem a few times and written something under each heading in your list, you should then try to say why the poet has written it in this way. For example, if the poem has a slow-flowing rhythm, why has the poet chosen this? If the poet has used alliteration, why are certain sounds emphasised?

Read the following poem by the twentieth-century poet, Kathleen Raine, and make a list of headings.

Now write notes about the poem under each of the headings. This is the first step towards writing more about the poem and what it means to you.

128

A Spell for Creation

Within the flower there lies a seed,
Within the seed there springs a tree,
Within the tree there spreads a wood.

In the wood there burns a fire,
And in the fire there melts a stone,
Within the stone a ring of iron.

Within the ring there lies an O,
Within the O there looks an eye,
In the eye there swims a sea,

And in the sea reflected sky,
And in the sky there shines the sun,
Within the sun a bird of gold.

Within the bird there beats a heart,
And from the heart there flows a song,
And in the song there sings a word.

In the word there speaks a world,
A world of joy, a world of grief,
From joy and grief there springs my love.

Oh love, my love, there springs a world,
And on the world there shines a sun,
And in the sun there burns a fire,

Within the fire consumes my heart,
And in my heart there beats a bird,
And in the bird there wakes an eye,
Within the eye, earth, sea and sky,
Earth, sky and sea within an O
Lie like the seed within the flower.

A Spell for Creation by Kathleen Raine

Poems

- When writing about a poem the most important thing is to read the poem out loud several times so you can hear the way the language works. Then you will be able to write about what the poem means to you.

summary

Questions

A

1. What does the layout of a poem refer to?
2. Why do poets use alliteration?
3. If we talk about the diction in a poem, what do we mean?
4. What is meant by the 'mood' of a poem?
5. Why is it a good idea to read a poem out loud?

B

1. What can you say about the layout of the poem 'A Spell for Creation'?
2. How does the poet create a sense of rhythm in this poem?
3. How has the poet written this poem to make it sound like a spell?
4. What images does the poet create in this spell?
5. A spell is normally used to create something magical. Why do you think the poet is using a spell in this poem?

C

Write about this poem, using your notes to say what poetic techniques have been used. Then go on to say whether you like the poem and what it means to you. Try to link up your ideas in paragraphs so that what you say about the language leads on to what you say about the meaning of the poem.

Writing Your Own Poems

intro

Many poems start off by painting a clear picture of a particular place, person, animal or object. The poet wants to get us interested and tries to arouse our curiosity or our emotions.

These pages are about helping you to get started with writing your own poetry.

Choosing the right words

One of the most important jobs in poetry is to choose the most effective words to express what you want to describe in a clear and interesting way. The nineteenth-century poet Samuel Taylor Coleridge wrote: 'Poetry = the best words in the best order.'

The modern poet Ted Hughes has written some advice about how to get started on a poem:

'Imagine what you are writing about. See it and live it ... look at it, touch it, smell it, listen to it, turn yourself into it ... keep your eyes, your ears, your nose, your taste, your touch, your whole being on the thing you are turning into words ... After a bit of practice, and after telling yourself a few times that you do not care how other people have written about this thing, this is the way you find it ... you will surprise yourself.'

from *Poetry in the Making* by Ted Hughes

One way to start a poem is to write down words and phrases that come into your head concerning the thing you are interested in. If, for example, you wanted to write a poem about the sun, you might start off like this:

[diagram: SUN in centre with branches to: summer & winter, sunrise (dawn) & sunset (dusk), holidays, new life, warm, yellow ball, huge star, blazing furnace, blinding brightness, millions of miles away]

You might then want to take one of these ideas and write about it in more detail or you might want to say something about all of them.

The modern poet Wes Magee wrote a poem called 'What Is the Sun?' in which he paints a picture of what the sun means to him.

What is the Sun?

*the sun is an orange dinghy
sailing across a calm sea*

*it is a gold coin
dropped down a drain in Heaven*

*the sun is a yellow beach ball
kicked high into the summer sky*

*it is a red thumb print
on a sheet of pale blue paper*

*the sun is a milk bottle's gold top
floating in a puddle*

What is the Sun? by Wes Magee

Look at how the poet has used **metaphors** (describing one thing as something else) to make the description more interesting and original. The metaphors also tell us how the poet feels about the sun.

Wes Magee has chosen a simple style for the poem with pairs of lines which allow him to concentrate on coming up with unusual ideas.

Once you have collected some words and phrases you can experiment with different styles. Look at the other poems in this book. Some of your poems could use rhyme and you could keep to a regular number of syllables in your lines.

Poems

summary

- When writing your own poetry start off by writing down words and phrases about something particular you are interested in. It does not matter what it is as long as it is important to you.
- It is a very good idea to try and use similes (see page 124) and metaphors to paint a clear picture of what you want to describe.
- Try out different patterns of arranging your words to see which works best.
- Think about ways of creating rhythm.

Look at the start to the poem 'Autumn Song' by Ted Hughes. Notice the way he repeats lines to give the poem a pattern. He also uses **personification** to make 'the day' seem human.

There came a day that caught the summer
Wrung its neck
Plucked it
And ate it.

Now what shall I do with the trees?
The day said, the day said.
Strip them bare, strip them bare.
Let's see what is really there.

And what shall I do with the sun?
The day said, the day said.
Roll him away till he's cold and small.
He'll come back rested if he comes back at all.

from *Autumn Song* by Ted Hughes

Questions

A

1. Why is it a good idea to use similes and metaphors in poetry?
2. Do you think it is a good idea to try to write a poem straight off or to make notes first?
3. How many metaphors has Wes Magee used in his poem?
4. What words does Ted Hughes repeat in his poem?
5. Does Ted Hughes use rhyme in his poem? If so, which lines rhyme?

B

1. Pick out one of the metaphors that Wes Magee uses and say what feelings it gives about the sun.
2. What pattern has Wes Magee used to start off the lines of his poem?
3. Pick out the pair of lines you find most interesting in this poem and say why you like them.
4. What pattern of lines does Ted Hughes use in his poem?
5. In the poem Ted Hughes describes the autumn day as if it was a living creature. Do you think this is an effective way to attract the reader's attention? Give your reasons.

C

1. Write your own poem in the style of 'What Is the Sun?', choosing from the following list:

   What Is the Moon?
   What Is the Sea?
   What Is a Tree?
   What Is a Bird?

2. Write your own poem about a season, describing it as if it was a living creature. Make notes about the season first, including the sights, sounds, colours and feelings you might have in this season. Then think of a person or a creature that you could compare it to.

For more information about metaphors see pages 124–125

Reading a Modern Play

intro

All plays are meant to be performed, either on television or radio, or live on stage. However, it is also very enjoyable and worthwhile to read playscripts, especially if you are able to read the parts out loud in a group.

These pages are about how to enjoy reading modern plays.

How to prepare a reading of a play

When you read a play you have more time to think about the characters and what they say and do. You can also imagine for yourself, how the actors might play the parts and how the play would be staged. In order to do this you might consider the following elements of plays:

- **The set**. This is how the play looks on the stage or screen – what scenery and furniture have been used and how the stage is organised.
- **Costumes**. Are they realistic/unusual/ historical/ futuristic?
- **Lighting**. Many different lighting effects can be used to highlight events, characters and atmosphere in the play.
- **Movement**. How do the characters move about the stage?
- **Sound**. Is music used or are there other sound effects?

Read the following extract from the play *A Game of Soldiers* by the modern writer Jan Needle. The play is set in the Falkland Islands during the Falklands War of 1982. Michael is 13, Thomas is 8, and together with Sarah they have found a wounded Argentinian soldier. They decide to kill him, but Sarah wants to give him some food before he dies.

The sea den. Michael and Thomas enter, talking.

Michael: (as they come in) It's great this, isn't it? It's not a game any more. It's real. Absolutely ace.

Thomas: Do you think she'll do it though? Do you think she'll go through with it?

Michael: She promised, didn't she? She swore like the rest of us? Death to the enemy! Fantastic.

Thomas: She only swore when you gave in though. It seems daft to me, to get him food and drink and blankets. Then to kill him. It's potty.

Michael: Female logic, Thomas. There's no rhyme or reason to it. But never mind, it does no harm to humour them. That's what my father always says.

Thomas: I could see her point in a way. I mean him with the gun and that. And us with nothing. It might lull him into a ... you know ... Mightn't it?

Michael: A sense of false security. Yeah, I s'pose it might. He might even go off to kip if he's got some food in him, and a nice warm blanket on. That'd make life easier. For us.

Thomas: (rather daring; he's subtly taunting Michael) And she didn't leave you a lot of choice, in the end, did she? Take it or leave it, she said, suit yourself. It was ....

Michael: Don't kid yourself son. I'd have talked her round. But she had a point, I've said so, haven't I? A sense of false security. (Pause)

Thomas: Michael?

H

When you read a play the dialogue and stage directions will be the most important things for you to focus on first. Speech and dialogue are the central features of all plays. They have to fulfil the following functions:

- Give you information about the characters.
- Establish what has already happened.
- Move the plot along.
- Tell you what the characters are thinking.
- Be lively and interesting so the audience is not bored.

Plays

Michael: Yeah?

Thomas: How you ... How we ... What exactly are we going to do? To ... you know ... kill him? ...

Michael: Well, there's lots of ways, aren't there? I mean, it would be easier if he didn't have a gun, we're going to have to be dead careful. Maybe we can let you sneak up on him and snatch the thing away.

Thomas: (horrified) What! Me! Sneak up on him!

Michael: (laughs) I'm pulling your leg, you twit. I wouldn't trust you to take a dummy off a baby. Relax.

Thomas: Crikey Michael. Don't say stuff like that! But what if he sees us coming, though? What if he shoots us?

Michael: He won't. That's why I agreed to let Nelly Knickerleg get the food and stuff. I might get my Mum's sleeping pills or something ...

Thomas: But what if they caught you at it?

Michael: They might. That's the problem. But I don't think it's necessary at all. I think we can do it easier, much easier. (He takes out his pen-knife and fingers it.) I don't half wish this was a real commando knife. That would be the easiest.

Thomas: Could you knife him, honestly? (pause, horrified) Groo, I'd throw up. I'd puke.

Michael: I'd stick it in his neck and pull. It'd be sharp as sharp. I'd slice it through his jugular and watch the blood squirt. I could do it.

Thomas: Hell, Michael. That's horrible.

from *A Game of Soldiers*
by Jan Needle

● When you read a modern play look closely at the dialogue and try to work out what the characters are thinking and feeling. Try to imagine how the play will look.

summary

Questions

A

1. Name three things that dialogue in a play is meant to do.
2. Why might it be useful to read a play before going to see it?
3. When you read a play why might it be a good idea to imagine what it would look like on stage?

B

1. In the extract from *A Game Of Soldiers* how does Michael feel about killing the soldier? Find some lines to back up your answer.
2. Does Thomas feel the same way? Explain why/why not.
3. Even though we do not see the girl Sarah, we are told certain things about her. What do we find out about her?
4. Look again at the things Michael says, especially about Sarah and about killing the soldier. What sort of a boy is Michael? Do you think he is as brave as he makes out? Give reasons for your answer.
5. Do you think the children will commit the killing? Say why you think they will/will not.

C

1. Imagine you are able to ask Sarah some questions about the situation the three children are in. Write an interview with her in which you try to find out as much as you can about what she thinks of the two boys and what she thinks they should all do.
2. Write your own continuation to this scene in which Sarah returns and they have to make a decision about what to do.

Writing Dialogue and Script

intro — Plays involve characters who are acting out a certain situation. This situation can be funny or sad, tense or light-hearted. When you write a playscript you need to plan out carefully what the situation will be and who the characters are.

> These pages are about how to write dialogue for a playscript.

Keeping things simple

It is a good idea not to make the situation too complicated, although a variety of different things happening will keep the audience interested.
It is also a good idea not to have too many speaking characters so the audience will not become confused.

Deciding on characters

When you have decided on a situation and who your characters are, you will need to make detailed notes about these characters so that you can make them as realistic as possible. This way, when they speak, the dialogue will sound realistic. Your notes should include:

- how old they are
- whether they are married and have children
- what job they do if they are employed
- what sort of personality they have
- any other unusual features.

Characters need to be as realistic as possible within the play even if they are fantasy or science-fiction characters. When you have a clear picture of your characters you will be able to show how they react in a particular situation and what they say to each other. You will then have a scene in your play.

Read the following extract from the play, *A Proper Little Nooryeff,* by the modern writer Leonard Gregory, based on the novel by Jean Ure. In this scene Anita and Jamie are in the rehearsal room at a dancing school. Anita is waiting enthusiastically for the dance lesson to begin but Jamie, who is a very talented dancer, has not even got changed yet.

Anita: What's the matter with you? Why haven't you got changed? (Pause) Jamie, Miss Tucker's going to be here any minute. You know she doesn't like wasting time. We have come here to dance, you know!

Jamie: Is that all you ever think about? Dancing?

Anita: No of course it isn't! But just at this moment ...

Jamie: So what else do you think about?

Anita: Lots of things. Loads of things!

Jamie: Do you ever think about the bomb and people starving and what it's like not to have money?

Anita: Well how often do you?

Jamie: More than you I bet. Do you know? I've never heard you talk about anything that wasn't ballet.

Anita: It's not because I'm not interested in other things. It's just that if you want to be a dancer there simply isn't room for anything else. If you really want to get anywhere ...

Jamie: Crap!

Anita: Jamie, it's not crap! It's true! Imagine if you wanted to be a footballer, or a cricketer, or a ... pop star, or something. Imagine how hard you'd have to work ... all those training sessions — all the practice. Well, it's exactly the same with dancing. It's no use thinking you can skip class every time you're feeling a bit off or something a bit more interesting turns up. You have to put ballet first ...

Jamie: This dancing lark. My Dad ...(Anita waits) My Dad reckons dancers are a load of old nannies.

Anita: Oh, well! Your Dad! It's the sort of stupid thing someone's Dad would say, isn't it? I bet your Dad doesn't know the first thing about it ... I bet he couldn't tell an 'entrechat' from an 'arabesque'. (Jamie says nothing) I suppose it would be all right if you wanted to be a boxer. That's manly, isn't it?
Two men knocking the life out of each other ...

Plays

Just as a story has different sections – introduction and setting; development and conflict; ending – so too will a play. These sections are called **scenes**.

summary

When writing dialogue for a playscript you need to think about:
- situation
- character
- how the play will look to the audience.

Questions

A

1. Name three things you need to consider when writing a playscript. For each one say why it is important and how it will help the play to be effective.
2. Why do you need to make notes on the characters in your play before writing any dialogue?
3. Why is it important for dialogue to be realistic?

B

1. In the extract from *A Proper Little Nooryeff* what starts off the argument between the two characters?
2. Which character do you sympathise most with and why?
3. Do you think the dialogue in this scene is realistic? How do you think the writer has done this?
4. From the way the characters talk do you think Anita is going to persuade Jamie to take his dancing more seriously? Give examples from the extract to back up your answer.

C

1. Write the character notes for Jamie and Anita that you think the writer will have made before he wrote this scene. You will need to include as much detail as you can about these two people, how old they are, what they look like, hobbies and interests, personality, etc.
2. Write your own scene where two people have an argument or a disagreement about something. You will first need to plan the scene carefully making detailed notes about the situation and the characters.

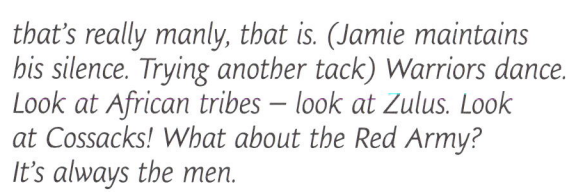

that's really manly, that is. (Jamie maintains his silence. Trying another tack) Warriors dance. Look at African tribes – look at Zulus. Look at Cossacks! What about the Red Army? It's always the men.

Jamie: *It's different for them.*

from *A Proper Little Nooryeff* by Leonard Gregory

Notice how the writer has made the dialogue seem realistic – the characters come across as real people in a real situation.

135

Reading Shakespeare

intro

When reading a Shakespeare play, remember that it was written to be performed. If you're at home, read it aloud, perhaps with a friend. Imagine how it might be acted. You could even try acting a scene, as well as picturing the costumes and scenery.

These pages will help you to understand and enjoy Shakespeare by teaching you about types of play, staging, storylines, acts and scenes, and characters.

Types of play

You will probably study one of three types of play. Each has its own characteristics:

- **Comedy** – humour, confusion, trickery and disguise, with people unhappily in love, but with happy endings and marriages.
- **Tragedy** – arguments and fights involving a noble hero who eventually dies.
- **History** – Shakespeare's version of real historical events and characters.

Acts and scenes

A Shakespeare play is in five **acts**, which are like chapters. Act 1 introduces the main characters and the storyline. Act 3 usually has the most exciting action in the story. Act 5 deals with the final conflict or misunderstanding, ending with deaths or weddings.

Acts are divided into **scenes**. Each scene is set in a single place. **Stage directions** at the start may tell you where this is. They will also tell you who is present, and when they **enter** and **exit**.

Getting into scenes and speeches

When reading a scene, ask yourself the following:

- *Where* is it set, and how does this fit the action?
- *Who* is in the scene, and when do they enter and exit?
- *What* do the characters think and feel about each other?
- *How* does the scene move the story on?

When focusing on a speech, ask yourself these questions:

- *Who* is speaking, and who to – or is the character 'thinking aloud'?
- *What* has just been happening?
- *How* does it fit the character?

Read the following extract from *Twelfth Night*. Olivia is a rich noblewoman, Malvolio her conceited and bossy chief servant. Olivia's maid-servant, Maria, has forged a letter from Olivia to trick Malvolio into thinking Olivia wants to marry him. The letter asks him to be proud, smile a lot and dress in a certain way. Malvolio quotes from the letter. Olivia thinks Malvolio must be ill.

Shakespeare

Olivia:	Wilt thou go to bed, Malvolio?
Malvolio:	To bed? Ay, sweetheart, and I'll come to thee.
Oliv:	God comfort thee! Why dost thou smile so, and kiss thy hand so oft?...
Maria:	Why appear you with this ridiculous boldness before my lady?
Mal:	'Be not afraid of greatness': 'twas well writ.
Oliv:	What mean'st thou by that, Malvolio?
Mal:	'Some are born great' –
Oliv:	Ha?
Mal:	'Some achieve greatness' –
Oliv:	What say'st thou?
Mal:	'And some have greatness thrust upon them.'
Oliv:	Heaven restore thee!
Mal:	'Remember who commended thy yellow stockings' –
Oliv:	Thy yellow stockings?
Mal:	'And wished to see thee cross-gartered.'
Oliv:	Cross-gartered?
Mal:	'Go to, thou art made, if thou desir'st to be so:' –
Oliv:	Am I made?
Mal:	'If not, let me see thee a servant still.'
Oliv:	Why, this is very midsummer madness.

commended = praised
thou art made = you've got it made (he'll be rich if he marries Olivia)

summary

- Shakespeare's plays are meant to be performed. Read them aloud.
- Shakespeare wrote comedies, tragedies and histories.
- If reading a scene or speech, think: Where? Who? What? How?

Questions

A
1. Name three types of Shakespeare play.
2. What type do you think *Twelfth Night* is? Give your reasons.
3. How is a Shakespeare play divided up?
4. Name two things that stage directions do.

B
1. Write out the lines that Malvolio quotes from the letter.
2. How would Malvolio 'achieve greatness' by marrying Olivia?
3. Olivia thinks at first that Malvolio must be ill. Explain (a) what misunderstanding arises from this, (b) what other misunder-standing comes near the end of the extract, and (c) what Olivia eventually thinks.

C
1. Use 'Getting into scenes and speeches' to help you comment on the extract.
2. Explain what an audience would find funny in this scene, and how you would direct each actor to speak and behave for best effect.

For more information about Shakespeare's language see pages 138–139

Shakespeare's Language

intro

English has changed since Shakespeare was alive. For example, he sometimes uses 'thy' for 'your', and 'thee' for 'you' or 'yourself'. Also, he was not trying to make his characters speak in an ordinary way: most of their speeches are in **verse**, and the language they use is **poetic**. The verse is **blank verse**, meaning that it does not rhyme.

These pages will help you to understand and enjoy Shakespeare's language, especially his use of verse and imagery.

Reading a speech

When reading a speech, think about how it fits into the scene, who is speaking and what the speech tells us about them, and what the mood of the speech is. Now read the speech by Lady Macbeth in the play *Macbeth*. A letter from her husband, Macbeth, has made her decide that King Duncan must die.

> Come, you spirits
> That tend on mortal thoughts! unsex me here,
> And fill me from the crown to the toe top-full
> Of direst cruelty; make thick my blood,
> Stop up the access and passage to remorse,
> That no compunctious visitings of nature
> Shake my fell purpose, nor keep peace between
> Th'effect and it! Come to my woman's breasts,
> And take my milk for gall, you murdering
>   ministers,
> Wherever in your sightless substances
> You wait on nature's mischief! Come, thick night,
> And pall thee in the dunnest smoke of hell,
> That my keen knife see not the wound it makes,
> Nor heaven peep through the blanket of the dark,
> To cry, 'Hold, hold!'

tend = wait
unsex me = take away my womanliness
direst = worst
Stop up… = 'Stop feelings of pity from upsetting my evil plans.'
gall = bitter fluid
sightless = blind
pall thee = cover yourself

Verse

You might notice that the speech has a regular **metre**. This means that most lines contain the same number of **syllables**. A syllable is the smallest part of a word you can pronounce on its own. In Shakespeare's verse they come in pairs:

'That my keen knife see not the wound it makes.'

Read this line tapping out the time with your finger. Count the pairs of syllables – there are five: de dum, de dum, de dum, de dum, de dum.

Variations in metre add to the meaning by making us pause or give extra weight to one word. For example, the line, *'And fill me from the crown to the toe top-full'* is itself overfull of syllables, making us give extra weight to *'toe top-full'*.

> **Shakespeare's verse is written in sentences. The end of a line is not necessarily the end of a sentence. Follow the sentence structure, not just the lines.**

Word pictures

An important part of Shakespeare's language is his **imagery**. An **image** is a kind of word picture that expresses an idea. One example in Lady Macbeth's speech is the image of darkness as a blanket, which heaven might 'peep' through.

Lady Macbeth **personifies** night (speaks as if it were a person), asking it to hide her deed. Macbeth does the same thing when he later decides to murder his friend Banquo.

> *Come, seeling night,*
> *Scarf up the tender eye of pitiful day,*
> *And with thy bloody and invisible hand*
> *Cancel and tear to pieces that great bond*
> *Which keeps me pale! Light thickens, and the crow*
> *Makes wing to the rooky wood;*
> *Good things of day begin to droop and drowse,*
> *Whiles night's black agents to their preys do rouse.*

summary

- Shakespeare usually writes in blank verse, with five pairs of syllables to a line.
- His imagery – word pictures – brings ideas to life. One kind of imagery is personification – speaking about a thing as if it were a person.

Questions

A
1. What is meant by metre?
2. Why is Shakespeare's verse called blank verse?
3. How many syllables are there in the word 'substances'?
4. Find three images in Lady Macbeth's speech.

B
1. What two phrases does Lady Macbeth use for the forces of evil?
2. Compare how she shows heaven and hell. Which seems more powerful? Why?
3. Describe how you think the speech should be acted.
4. Compare how Macbeth and Lady Macbeth are feeling in these speeches, by referring in detail to the language used in both.

C
1. Draw the images in Macbeth's speech, or in another Shakespeare speech, as you imagine them.
2. Write about another Shakespeare speech of at least 15 lines. Comment on (a) mood, (b) use of imagery and any other use of words that strikes you, and (c) what the language tells you about the character.

For more information about verse see pages 120–121

Writing About Shakespeare's Characters

intro

To understand a character and know what to write, ask yourself the questions on this page (C = character). Find evidence to support your answers. When writing, use short quotations if they help to make your point, or use your own words to refer to a speech or part of the scene.

These pages explain how asking the right questions can help you to write about a Shakespeare character.

- How does C want to be seen by others?
- How *is* C seen by others?
- What does C want?
- What does C fear?
- What does C do, if anything, in the scene?
- How does C react to, and treat, others?
- How does C's attitude and mood change as the scene progresses?
- How is C's personality revealed overall? For example, is C loyal, brave, honest, vain?

In this scene from *Julius Caesar*, Caesar's wife Calphurnia has persuaded him not to go to the Senate House. When Decius comes to fetch him, she suggests an excuse. The audience knows that Decius and others plan to kill Caesar at the Senate House.

Calphurnia: Say he is sick.

Caesar: Shall Caesar send a lie?
Have I in conquest stretched mine arm so far,
To be afeard to tell greybeards the truth?
Decius, go tell them Caesar will not come.

Decius: Most mighty Caesar, let me know some cause,
Lest I be laughed at when I tell them so.

Shakespeare

Caes: The cause is in my will: I will not come.
 That is enough to satisfy the Senate.
 But for your private satisfaction,
 Because I love you, I will let you know:
 Calphurnia here, my wife, stays me at home.
 She dreamt tonight she saw my statua,
 Which, like a fountain with an hundred spouts,
 Did run pure blood; and many lusty Romans
 Came smiling and did bathe their hands in it.
 And these does she apply for warnings and portents
 And evils imminent, and on her knee
 Hath begged that I will stay at home today.

Dec: This dream is all amiss interpreted;
 It was a vision fair and fortunate.
 Your statue spouting blood in many pipes,
 In which so many smiling Romans bathed,
 Signifies that from you great Rome shall suck
 Reviving blood, and that great men shall press
 For tinctures, stains, relics, and cognizance.
 This by Calphurnia's dream is signified.

Caes: And this way have you well expounded it.

Dec: I have, when you have heard what I can say —
 And know it now: the Senate have concluded
 To give this day a crown to mighty Caesar.
 If you shall send them word you will not come,
 Their minds may change. Besides it were a mock
 Apt to be rendered, for some one to say
 'Break up the Senate till another time,
 When Caesar's wife shall meet with better dreams'.
 If Caesar hide himself, shall they not whisper
  'Lo, Caesar is afraid'?
 Pardon me, Caesar; for my dear dear love
 To your proceeding bids me tell you this,
 And reason to my love is liable.

Caes: How foolish do your fears seem now, Calphurnia!
 I am ashamed I did yield to them.
 Give me my robe, for I will go.

portents = signs
imminent = coming
tinctures ... cognizance = handkerchiefs dipped in blood for souvenirs

- Ask the right questions. In particular, what does the character want and fear, and how does he or she behave towards others? Support your claims with evidence: short quotes or your own words.

summary

Questions

A

1 Which word tells us that the senators are old men?
2 What has Calphurnia dreamed?
3 How does Decius interpret it?
4 How does Decius try to get Caesar to go to the Senate House?
5 How does Caesar eventually describe Calphurnia's fears?

B

1 Answer the questions on character as they apply to Caesar in the extract.
2 What do you learn of Decius' character in this scene?

3 Draw three columns on a sheet of paper and write in the headings: Caesar, Decius, Calphurnia. Choose from the following list the words that you think best describe each character and put them in the columns. A word can fit more than one character, or it might fit none of them: proud; anxious; lazy; ambitious; two-faced; depressed; loyal; persuasive; trusting; inventive; noble; scornful; superstitious; brave; honest; insincere.

4 What does each quote below reveal about the speaker?
 'Say he is sick.'
 'Shall Caesar send a lie?'
 'Pardon me, Caesar; for my dear dear love...'

C

1 Explain Caesar's attitude at the start and how he is gradually persuaded.
2 Use the character questions to help you describe what another Shakespeare scene reveals about one character.

141

More About Shakespeare's Characters

intro

Sometimes, instead of being asked to write **about** a character, you may be asked to imagine that you **are** that character. This involves imagining how that character would feel. Practise by imagining you're someone you know — for example a relative or friend.

These pages aim to help you with creative writing tasks in which you have to put yourself in the position of a Shakespeare character.

Tips on getting into character

- Remind yourself — or find out — what has happened to your character so far.
- Move about and speak your character's lines aloud.
- Get someone to ask you how you (in character) are feeling. Tell them. If this is impossible, imagine that you're being interviewed.
- Bear in mind your character's sex, age and background, and that he or she is from Shakespeare's time, not now. Their attitudes may not always be the same as yours.

Read the two extracts from *Romeo and Juliet*. Romeo and Juliet are teenagers from feuding families. They have married in secret, but Romeo has just killed Juliet's cousin Tybalt, who first picked a fight with Romeo and then killed Romeo's friend Mercutio. For killing Tybalt, Romeo has been banished. Juliet hears the news from her nurse.

Juliet: O God! Did Romeo's hand shed Tybalt's blood?

Nurse: It did, it did, alas the day, it did.

Juliet: O serpent heart, hid with a flowering face.
Did ever dragon keep so fair a cave?
Beautiful tyrant, fiend angelical,
Dove-feathered raven, wolvish-ravening lamb!
Despised substance of divinest show!
Just opposite to what thou justly seem'st!
A damned saint, an honourable villain!
O nature what hadst thou to do in hell
When thou didst bower the spirit of a fiend
In mortal paradise of such sweet flesh?
Was ever book containing such vile matter
So fairly bound? O, that deceit should dwell
In such a gorgeous palace.

Nurse: There's no trust,
No faith, no honesty in men....
Shame come to Romeo.

Juliet: Blistered be thy tongue
For such a wish. He was not born to shame.
Upon his brow shame is ashamed to sit,
For 'tis a throne where honour may be crowned
Sole monarch of the universal earth.
O, what a beast was I to chide at him.

142

Shakespeare

In the second extract the nurse tells Romeo how Juliet has taken the news:

Romeo: Speak'st thou of Juliet? How is it with her?
Doth not she think me an old murderer
Now I have stained the childhood of our joy
With blood removed but little from her own?
Where is she? And how doth she? And what says
My concealed lady to our cancelled love?

Nurse: O, she says nothing, sir, but weeps and weeps,
And now falls on her bed, and then starts up,
And Tybalt calls, and then on Romeo cries,
And then down falls again.

Romeo: As if that name,
Shot from the deadly level of a gun,
Did murder her, as that name's cursed hand
Murdered her kinsman.

summary

- When writing about Shakespeare 'in character' you must imagine that you are the character. Think about their sex, age and background, and how they must be feeling.

Questions

A

Answer these questions as if you were either Romeo or Juliet.

1. Who was Tybalt?
2. Why have you married in secret?
3. Does it seem fair that Romeo has been banished?
4. What does Romeo mean by 'blood removed but little from her own'?
5. What have you got to be glad of?

B

1. Imagine you are Romeo or Juliet. Write about your feelings at this time. Notice the opposites in Juliet's first speech, such as 'dove-feathered raven'. For Romeo, think of the phrases 'stained', 'cancelled love' and 'cursed hand'.
2. Write a scene in modern English in which the lovers meet again and tell each other how they were feeling at first, and how they are feeling now.
3. Imagine you are either the Nurse or Friar Lawrence, who married the two lovers and advises Romeo. Write a letter of advice to one of the lovers.

C

The couple have their wedding night, but then Romeo must leave – because he's been banished. Then Juliet has a new problem: her father insists that she must marry another man – Paris. She dares not say that she's already married. Write her letter to a magazine problem page asking for help.

Common word confusions

intro

This page lists some commonly confused words and gives examples showing how they *should* be used.

accept / except
I accept what you say — except the bit about me being lazy.

access / excess
We couldn't gain access to our excess baggage.

affect / effect
Using margarine won't affect the taste, but engine grease could have a disastrous effect.

complement / compliment
Those colours really complement each other — but then I expect you're used to receiving compliments.

knew / new
I knew you'd like my new friend.

lead / led
Lead me where you led me yesterday. My head feels as heavy as lead.

licence / license
A TV licence (noun) doesn't license (verb) you to deafen the neighbours.

lose / loose
I'd hate to lose my loose change.

of / off / 've
If a friend of mine had got off the bus, I would've noticed. ('Would've' sounds like 'Would of', but means 'Would have'.)

passed / past
I passed (verb) her the fading photo — all that was left of the past (noun).

practise / practice
Practise (verb) your violin every day — practice (noun) makes perfect.

principal / principle
The principal reason for my returning your purse is that I'm a man of principle.

quiet / quite
Stay quiet and you'll be quite safe.

stationary / stationery
My car was stationary at the lights, so I jumped out to buy some writing paper in a stationery shop.

there / their / they're
Over there you'll find their names: they're all famous.

thorough / through
The girl was thorough in reading through her essay.

to / too / two
Go back to New York: this town's too small for the two of us.

uninterested / disinterested
I can tell by your yawning that you're uninterested in me. I have nothing to gain from the will — I'm a disinterested observer.

wear / we're / where
Wear something smart: we're going to a party — I don't know where.

who's / whose
Who's there? Whose voice is that?

your / you're
Your stories bore me, and you're making me late.

Mini-thesaurus

This page gives alternatives for some commonly overused words. Use these words to add variety to your writing. Many of the alternatives have slightly different meanings from each other, or can only be used in certain ways. For example, you could cook a 'nice' meal for a 'nice' person, or a 'delicious' meal for a 'nice' person - but probably not a 'nice' meal for a 'delicious' person! Therefore, you may need to use a dictionary as well.

all right
not bad, acceptable, tolerable, adequate, passable, bearable

bad
serious, appalling, terrible, awful, vile, loathsome, disgusting, obnoxious, horrid, horrible, dire

beautiful
pretty, attractive, lovely, exquisite, gorgeous, handsome, stunning, breathtaking

big
enormous, colossal, gigantic, huge, giant, gargantuan, outsize, vast, limitless

delicious
tasty, delectable, flavoursome

fat
large, plump, chunky, ample, well-built, well-rounded, fleshy

good
excellent, superb, wonderful, first-rate, brilliant, incomparable, unparalleled

nasty
cruel, foul, heartless, spiteful, evil, shameful, wicked, unforgivable

nice
pleasant, agreeable, pleasurable, enjoyable
(*see also* beautiful and good)

old
ancient, antique, well-worn, wrinkled, mature; (of something past) former, previous, ex-, last

poor
penniless, impoverished, humble, impecunious

pretty
lovely, quaint, pleasing, charming
(*see also* beautiful)

rich
well-heeled, wealthy, affluent, well-off, prosperous

small
tiny, minute, minuscule, miniature, undersized, dwarfish

strange
odd, bizarre, peculiar, unusual, mysterious

thin
slender, slim, skinny, stick-like, emaciated

young
fresh, new, youthful, juvenile, immature

Further reading

Reading is the best way to improve your English skills. The more you read the more new words and ideas you will come across. You will also become familiar with new sentence structures and new ways of expressing yourself. If you want to be good at something you need to practise regularly, so try to read every day.

You should try to read as many different styles of writing as possible and always be prepared to give something a go, even if you are not sure whether you are going to like it. The following list contains suggestions in many different genres which will help you to understand the ideas discussed in the main sections of this book. Try to find some more titles of your own and see how they compare with the ones in this list.

If you come across a book that you particularly like, you may wish to write a review of it and send it to your local library or even to the author. It often helps you to get more out of a book if you write down your feelings about it. Read some book reviews in newspapers to see how they are written or look at pages 78 and 79 for help.

Literary Non-fiction

The Diary of Anne Frank	Anne Frank
Zlata's Diary	Zlata Filipovic
The Groucho Letters	Groucho Marx
The Diaries of Samuel Pepys	Samuel Pepys
Catch Me a Colobus	Gerald Durrell
My Family and Other Animals	Gerald Durrell
The Kon Tiki Expedition	Thor Heyerdahl

There are many biographies and autobiographies about famous people (including pop stars, sports personalities, film and TV stars) that you can read, depending on your interests.

Prose

Modern novels

Underrunners	Margaret Mahy
The Haunting	Margaret Mahy
The Kingdom by the Sea	Robert Westall
A Place for Me	Robert Westall
The Granny Project	Anne Fine
Madame Doubtfire	Anne Fine
The Pinballs	Betsy Byars
Back Home	Michelle Magorian
Carrie's War	Nina Bawden
My Family and Other Natural Disasters	Josephine Feeney
Night Fires	Joan Lingard
Follow A Shadow	Robert Swindells

Older novels

Great Expectations	Charles Dickens
Oliver Twist	Charles Dickens
A Christmas Carol	Charles Dickens
Huckleberry Finn	Mark Twain
Tom Sawyer	Mark Twain
The War of the Worlds	H. G. Wells
Around the World in 80 Days	Jules Verne

Further reading

Poetry

There's a Poet Behind You	edited by Morag Styles & Helen Cook
Laughter is An Egg	John Agard
You Wait Till I'm Older Than You	Michael Rosen
The Puffin Book of Classic Verse	edited by Raymond Wilson
Comic Verse	edited by Roger McGough
The Rattlebag	edited by Ted Hughes & Seamus Heaney

Plays

A Game of Soldiers	Jan Needle
The Monster Garden	Diane Samuels
The Silver Sword	Stuart Henson
A Proper Little Nooryeff	Leonard Gregory
The Cuckoo Sister	Vivien Alcock
Under Milk Wood	Dylan Thomas

The most important thing to do when reading any book is to enjoy it!

Shakespeare

Any of the plays, in particular:

Macbeth
Romeo and Juliet
A Midsummer Night's Dream

Also as a useful introduction:

Illustrated Tales from Shakespeare	Adapted from Charles & Mary Lamb
The World of Shakespeare	Anna Claybourne & Rebecca Treays

Glossary

Words in italic have their own separate entry

abstract noun	a word referring to a thing that cannot be seen or touched: e.g. 'love' or 'freedom'.
accent	the way in which someone pronounces words, depending on their social background and where they come from.
Act	a part of a play. A Shakespeare play is divided into five Acts.
adjective	a word used to describe a *noun*: e.g. 'big' or 'beautiful'.
adverb	a word added to an adjective or (more often) a verb, as in '<u>very</u> happy' or 'Go <u>quickly</u>.'
alliteration	repetition of a sound, normally at the beginnings of words, as in 'deep, dark dungeon'.
Anglo-Saxon	the language spoken by most people in England before the Norman Conquest, which began in 1066.
antonym	a word opposite in meaning to another one.
atmosphere	the mood produced by a piece of writing.
auxiliary verb	a 'helping' *verb* used in the *tenses* of other verbs: e.g. 'I <u>have</u> spoken.'
bias	one-sidedness in presenting *facts* or arguments.
caricature	in a novel or play, a portrayal of a character which exaggerates certain features, often humorously.
clause	a group of words forming part of a sentence, including a subject and something said about it: e.g. 'The dog was hungry.'
cliffhanger	a dramatic ending to an episode of a drama or serialised novel which makes the audience keen to know what happens next.
closed question	a question which invites a 'yes/no' answer: e.g. 'Are you married?'
collective noun	a singular *noun* referring to a number of individuals: e.g. family.
colloquial	as used in everyday, informal speech: e.g. 'Hi! How's it going?'
comedy	(1) anything meant to be funny; (2) a particular kind of Shakespeare play which has a lot of humour and confusion, and a happy ending.
common nouns	words used to label things, people and animals: e.g. bat, door, skateboard.
compound word	a word made up of two words: e.g. spellcheck, dogfight, schoolgirl.
conjunction	a word that joins other words or phrases together: e.g. and, but, or.
consonant	any letter other than a, e, i, o, u.
contraction	a word made by running two words together and replacing missing letters with an apostrophe: e.g. can't, don't would've.

Glossary

deictic	a pointing word, as in 'that woman'.	**idiom**	a phrase with an established meaning that is not clear from the individual words: e.g. 'The lads were gutted.'
derivation	the origin of a word.		
Dewey Decimal System	a method of organising library books (see pages 58–59).	**image**	a word picture used to bring an idea to life: e.g. a *metaphor*, *simile* or *personification*.
dialect	a local version of English (or another language) with some differences of grammar and *vocabulary* from the standard form.	**imagery**	the kind of word picture used to bring an idea to life.
		infinitive	the open-ended form of a *verb*: e.g. to laugh, to cry, to listen.
dialogue	conversation between two or more people.	**informal**	the opposite of *formal*.
direct speech	the actual words someone says, given in quotation marks.	**interrogative**	a word which asks a question: e.g. what, who, why.
draft	(1) to produce a piece of writing that you expect to improve (redraft) later; (2) the piece of writing itself, as in: 'My final draft is easier to read.'	**intonation**	the musical rise and fall of speech.
		layout	the way words are set out on a page.
		legend	an old story originally based on something which actually happened.
emotive language	words used to stir up the reader's emotions.	**metaphor**	a description of a thing or action as if it were something else that is somehow similar: e.g. 'My home is my castle'; 'You're fishing for compliments.'
etymology	the way a word and its meaning have changed over time.		
fact	a piece of information generally accepted as true and usually provable.	**metre**	in poetry, a set rhythm determined by the pattern of *syllables* in a line.
fiction	something which is made up.		
flashback	in a novel or drama, a scene which goes back in time.	**mnemonic**	something which helps your memory.
formal	the more careful, serious style in which we speak or write when addressing people we do not know well, or when we want to show respect or be taken seriously.	**monologue**	a speech given by one character.

myth	an ancient story, often about gods and strange creatures, that has changed over the centuries in being handed down by word of mouth.	**preposition**	a small word coming before a *noun* or *pronoun*: e.g. <u>to</u> market; <u>on</u> time.
mythology	(1) the study of *myths*; (2) a collection of myths from a particular area, or relating to a particular god or creature.	**pronoun**	a word taking the place of a *noun*: e.g. I, her, our, myself, who, these.
		pronunciation	the way in which someone speaks.
narrative	a story, or something in story form: e.g. a narrative poem. 'First person' narrative is told as if someone is telling us his or her story directly ('I went …'). 'Third person' narrative is told as if by an observer ('She went …').	**register**	the form or style of English used in a particular situation, especially *formal* or *informal*.
		review	(1) to look at something again; (2) a piece of writing judging a performance, work of art, piece of music, play, novel, etc.
noun	a 'thing' word: e.g. boy, girl, fish, life, Africa.	**rhyming couplet**	in poetry, a pair of rhyming lines.
Old English	see *Anglo-Saxon*.	**rhyming slang**	in Cockney English, a system of replacing words with phrases that rhyme with them: e.g. 'butcher's hook' (or just 'butcher's') for 'look'.
onomatopoeia	a word which echoes the sound to which it refers: e.g. ping-pong.		
open question	a question which cannot be answered by 'yes' or 'no'.	**scene**	a division of a play, within an *Act*, in which all the action occurs in one place.
opinion	a personal viewpoint.		
participle	a word formed from a *verb*: e.g. going, gone, been.	**set**	in the theatre, the scenery, furniture, etc., on stage.
personification	a description of something (e.g. sleep) as if it were a person.	**setting**	the place where part of a story unfolds: e.g. a garden.
plot	the story of a work of fiction.	**simile**	a comparison of two things which are different in most ways but similar in one significant way: e.g. 'Her mouth closed like a steel trap.'
prefix	something which comes at the beginning of a word and which affects the meaning of what comes after: e.g. <u>pre</u>- as in 'pre-arranged signal' or 'pre-school child'.		
		slang	casual, often humorous, language used within a particular social group.

Glossary

standard English — the English most readily understood by all speakers of English, used especially in *formal* situations and by anyone speaking to strangers or the public (e.g. politicians or newsreaders).

stanza — a verse of a poem.

suffix — something coming at the end of a word and affecting its meaning in a set way: e.g. <u>ism</u> in Hinduism or Judaism; <u>itis</u> in tonsillitis or school-itis.

syllable — the smallest pronounceable part of a word. 'Fish' has one syllable; 'fishing' has two.

synonym — a word meaning the same as another word.

target audience — the typical reader or viewer at which a piece or writing, television programme or advertisement is aimed.

tense — the time element of a *verb*: e.g. 'I go' (present tense), 'I will go' (future tense).

theme — an idea explored throughout a piece of writing: e.g. loyalty.

tragedy — in drama (especially Shakespeare) a play where the main character suffers and usually dies at the end.

verb — sometimes described as 'doing' words; verbs are words which can express a wide range of meanings, such as actions, sensations, or states of being.

vocabulary — individual words used, as opposed to grammar.

vowel — a, e, i, o, u.

Index

abbreviations 33
abstract nouns 20, 21
accent 2–3
active listening 46, 47
active verbs 24, 25
adjectival clauses 30–31
adjectives 13, 20–21, 22, 23, 78
adverbial clauses 30–31
adverbial phrases 28
adverbs 13, 24, 25, 28
adverbs of degree 21, 23
advertisements 88–95
advice material 94–95
alliteration 124, 125, 128, 129
Anglo-Saxons 10
antonyms 17
apostrophes 34, 35
atmosphere 114–115
articles 20, 21, 23
audience 41, 52–53, 54–55, 90, 91
authoring skills 40–45
author's voice 117
autobiography 38–39, 98–99
auxiliary verbs 26, 27

bar graphs 64
bias 84–85
biography 98–99
book reviews 78, 79

capital letters 32–33
caricature 111
catalogues 59
CD-ROMs 60
Celts 10
characters
   plays 132, 134–135
   prose 102–103, 110–111, 118
   Shakepeare 140–143
charities 92–93, 94, 95
charts 64, 66–67
clauses 30–31, 32, 33, 35
clichés 87
close reading 57
collective nouns 20, 21
colons 34, 35
commas 32, 33
common nouns 20, 21
comparatives 20–21
comparison 29
complex sentences 30–31
compound sentences 29
compound words 18, 19
computers 45
confidence 52–53
conjunctions 29
connectives 29, 31, 39

consonants 12, 18, 19
continuous tenses 27
cooperation 50–51
coordinated complex sentences 31

definite article 20
deictic adjectives 20
deictic pronouns 22
description 20–21, 78, 79, 114–115, 116–117, 118–119
Dewey Decimal System 58–59
diagrams 66–67
dialect 2–3, 26–27
dialogue 132, 133, 134–135
diaries 96, 97, 100, 101, 117
diction 128, 129
dictionaries 11, 16, 17, 58
direct speech 32, 33, 36–37
doubling rule 12, 13
drafting 43

editorials 86, 87
editors, letters to 74–75
emotive language 84, 85, 92–93
encyclopedias 58, 60
essays, planning 42–43
exaggeration 84, 85, 110–111
exclamation marks 32–33

facts 82–83
factual statements 82, 83
fiction 58, 59
film reviews 78, 79
flow charts 66–67
foreign words 6, 11
formal letters 72, 73
formal register 4–5
full stops 32–33
future tense 24, 25, 26–27

grammar 20–31
   dialect 2
   nouns, articles and adjectives 20–21
   pronouns and noun phrases 22–23
   sentences 28–31
   verbs 24–27
graphs 64
group work 50–51

half rhyme 126, 127
handwriting 45
hyphens 18

idioms 2, 3
image 90, 91
imagery 124–125, 128, 129, 139
indefinite article 20

indefinite pronouns 22
indexes 16, 56, 59
infinitives 27
informal letters 73
informal register 4–5
information
   charts, graphs and tables 64–65
   instructions 66–67
   notes and summaries 62–63
   posters 68–69
   reports 70–71
   researching 60–61
instructions 66–67
Internet 60
interrogative adjectives 20
interrogative pronouns 22
interviewing 48–49
intonation 2, 3, 52
inverted commas 36–37

Latin 10, 11
layout 128, 129
leaflets 95
legends 108–109
letter patterns 14
letters 72–75, 97, 117
library 58–59
listening 46–47, 48–49, 50
lists 32, 33, 35, 62
literature
   non-fiction 96–101
   plays 132–143
   poems 120–131
   prose 102–119
   Shakespeare 136–143
logical connectives 31

main clauses 30, 31
memory tricks 15
metaphors 124, 125, 130, 131
metre 139
missing letters 34, 35
mnemonics 15
monologue 9
mood 128, 129
music reviews 78, 79
myths 106–107

narrative technique 116–117, 118
narrative writing 38, 39
   see also non-fiction; prose
news reports 80–81
newspapers 60, 74–75, 80–87
non-fiction 58, 59, 60, 96–101
   biography and autobiography 98–99
   diaries and letters 96–97
   travel writing 100–101
Normans 11
notebook 14, 15